RESTLESS CHURCHES

RESTLESS CHURCHES
How Canada's Churches Can Contribute
to the Emerging Religious Renaissance

Reginald W. Bibby

WOOD LAKE BOOKS

NOVALIS

© 2004 by Reginald Bibby

Cover design: Caroline Gagnon
Cover image: Whit Slemmons
Text design: Andrew Smith/Page Wave Graphics Inc.
Layout: Richard Proulx

Published in 2004 by Novalis/Saint Paul University
Business Office:
49 Front Street East, 2nd Floor
Toronto, Ontario, Canada
M5E 1B3

Phone: 1-877-702-7773 or (416) 363-3303
Fax: 1-877-702-7775 or (416) 363-9409
E-mail: cservice@novalis.ca
www.novalis.ca

Wood Lake Books
9025 Jim Bailey Road
Kelowna, British Columbia
V4V 1R2

Phone: 1-800-663-2775 or (250) 766-2778
E-mail: info@woodlake.com
www.woodlakebooks.com

Library and Archives Canada Cataloguing in Publication

Bibby, Reginald W.
Restless churches : how Canada's churches can contribute
to the emerging religious renaissance / Reginald W. Bibby.

Includes bibliographical references and index.
ISBN 2-89507-518-2

1. Canada–Religion–21st century. I. Title.

BL2530.C3B525 2004   306.6'0971   C2004-904284-X

Printed in Canada.

We acknowledge the financial support of the Government of Canada through the Book
Publishing Industry Development Program (BPIDP) for our publishing activities.

5 4 3 2 1   08 07 06 05 04

Contents

Dedication

To Three Very Special Women

Margaret,
Lolita, &
Sahara

Preface

I love ideas. And although it was never a part of my original biographical game plan, I have been given the opportunity of spending most of my life being paid to think and to share my thoughts with others to an extent beyond anything I ever could have imagined. Sometimes in the past I have joked to people that I hoped someone would etch on my tombstone, "He made people think."

But I love life more. As a result, for me the perfect synthesis is for good ideas to inform life so that living can be enhanced. Ideas that enrich life and elevate spirits are the ideas I enjoy most.

So it is that this book represents an effort to present good ideas about religious developments in Canada, ideas that are based on a large body of available research that consists of my life's work as well as the contributions of others. However, the book is an attempt to do much more. The findings have extremely important implications for what religious groups that are committed to effective ministry to Canadians need to be doing. What I am attempting to do is to present the key findings with clarity, reflect on some of the major implications, acknowledge a number of significant hurdles that have to be cleared, and spell out some of the tangible responses that groups need to consider.

My hope is that the result will be enhanced ministry and enriched living for all involved. My obvious assumption is that faith potentially has much to add to individual lives and to collective life. That contribution needs to be made through religious groups that see reality clearly and minister soundly.

This book, like my previous books, is anything but a one-person effort. More than 20,000 adults and teenagers have participated in ten national surveys dating back to 1975 and have contributed much to what we currently know about religion in Canada. My debt to those people is enormous. But data need interpretation and clarification, and possible implications require considerable thought and reflection. Over the past three decades an exceptionally large number of individuals in a wide array of religious group and academic settings have offered their thoughts, teaching me much, and contributing immensely to my effort to make sense of the research findings. In the last year or so, for example, I have benefited greatly from discussing the material with faculty and students at a number of universities besides my own, including Acadia, McMaster, the Vancouver School of Theology, St. Jerome's, and Assumption. I have had the privilege of appearing at many cross-group events, as well as at an array of specific United, Anglican, Lutheran, Presbyterian, Roman Catholic, and evangelical gatherings. On occasion I also have met one on one with religious officials. That overall collective input should be evident in the pages that follow.

I continue to be so very grateful to the Lilly Endowment, and to Craig Dykstra, Jim Lewis, and Chris Coble, for the generous funding that has made much of the data collection possible. My gratitude to the University of Lethbridge for resources, emotional support, and tranquility remains immense. The enthusiastic encouragement and manuscript assistance provided by Michael O'Hearn, Kevin Burns, and Anne Louise Mahoney at Novalis has made the writing of the book an enjoyable experience.

Finally, I want to express my deep appreciation to my family for their ongoing support – my three guys, Reggie, Dave, and Russ and, this time around, particularly to the three prominent women in my life: my mother, Margaret, whose valuing of faith and gratitude for life from the confines of her nursing home room inspired and invigorated me daily; my wife, Lita, whose consistent support simply makes life better and easier; and the person who just about never made it into this world, my little daughter Sahara Margaret – who, through her joyful presence and life-giving impact, poignantly symbolizes the mysteriousness and goodness of God.

My hope is that this book will result in enacted ideas that will likewise attest to the activity of such a God, and in the process elevate life for all Canadians.

REGINALD W. BIBBY
Lethbridge, Alberta
August 2004

Confessions of a Sociologist

It's interesting how academic life can sometimes have the effect of closing one's mind rather than opening it. When one sells one's soul to the scientific method of making sense of what is, part of the bargain is that one agrees to limit "what is" to what can be known empirically through the senses. A second part of the deal is that budding scientists are taught to focus on facts rather than dabble in implications and responses. One's role is to call things the way they are and leave the responses to those who are directly involved. Similar to the sports analyst up in the booth, the scientific observer watches, describes, and explains what's happening. But responsibility for changes in the game lies with the players and their coaches – people and their leaders.

At this point in my life I have little patience with such an excessive price for my soul.

Beyond A-Theism: Allowing for "The God Factor"

To limit reality to the empirically observable is a pretty precarious posture when one is trying to study religion, with its central emphasis upon gods that seldom, if ever, make themselves known through the senses. To assume such an "a-theistic" position when studying religion and religious claims is to run the risk of eliminating too much of what is truly important. As I reminded readers in *Restless Gods* (2002 and 2004), to treat religion as if it is only a human phenomenon might be to ignore the key to understanding what is happening in reality's so-called observable realm. It's something like looking at the person on the ladder who

1

has just got an electric shock while screwing in a light bulb – and trying to describe what happened without being aware of the electricity.

While it is not scientific to *assume* that what people believe is true, or that what they think they are experiencing *is* in fact what is taking place, it's also not good science to assume these events can be explained solely by social and personal factors. In the case of the light-bulb shock, to take this approach would be to limit explanations to the person and fail to take into account the electric current. When people make claims involving the non-observable, such ideas and events may be due to (a) human factors only or (b) factors that cannot be empirically known, but nonetheless are real.

Consequently, it seems to me that a more sound – if more radical – approach to studying religion is to call things the way they are, but, when it comes to interpreting what we observe, to keep our minds open to the possibility of the importance of a non-observable "God factor." For example, if Canadians continue to claim, in numbers that readily exceed the number of people who are active in religious groups, that they experience God, it is worth considering that the sources of these experiences may not be limited to observable social and psychological factors. Maybe – just maybe – God is relating *directly* to people.

Can we demonstrate that scientifically? No. But as scientists, we can introduce such a "God hypothesis." What's more, if observable factors cannot readily account for the pervasiveness of experience claims, it's our responsibility to raise such a hypothesis. Here, as I noted in *Restless Gods*, we are recognizing with St. Augustine not only that our souls are restless, but also that we perhaps are being pursued by One who makes us restless. With historian Arnold Toynbee we recognize that the key to a full understanding of the world "is not limited to that part of it which is accessible to the human senses" but may lie "in that other part which is not accessible" to the senses.

There is an important point to all this. Those of you who are familiar with my work will find this book to be "theistically uninhibited." I myself am a theist. I believe in God and have known the presence of God in my own life for about as long as I can remember. What's more, I am continually in awe of the way in which God seems to be at work in everyday life – in my life and in the lives of others, in institutions and in events, in things immediate and things global. In view of the fact that I am writing this book primarily for a Christian audience, I see no reason to hold back in reflecting with you, most of whom likewise are believers, on some of the ways in which God may be working in Canada today.

Inclusion of "the God factor" makes for a story that's much more filled out, more interesting, and more accurate. *J(*

Beyond Observation: Exploring Implications and Responses

In my early years of chronicling the Canadian religious scene, I felt it was my role as a sociologist to simply call things the way they were and leave the implications and responses to others, notably church leaders – a posture that is readily evident in my book *Fragmented Gods* (1987). I would tell religious leaders things such as:

- Canadians aren't dropping out of religious groups.
- Conservative Protestant churches are growing primarily because they do a good job of holding on to their kids.
- Large numbers of Canadians are expecting religious rites of passage.

However, I quickly learned that, while people found such a one-hour presentation on "The Context of Ministry" interesting and they went away politely appreciative, most didn't seem to have a clue as to what the findings might mean for ministry. I like to live with at least the illusion that what I do matters. As a result, I expanded my one-hour presentations into two sessions: one on "The Context of Ministry," and the second on "Implications for Ministry." For example:

- I'd tell people in the first session about the *drop-out myth*, and in the second session I'd remind them that this means they have a better chance of initiating a conversation with those folks than anyone else.
- Having presented the findings on *how evangelical churches grow*, I would proceed to emphasize that if organized religious groups want to grow, they must hold on to their children and keep track of their geographically mobile affiliates. If they want to evangelize, the key is personal relationships.
- I built on my findings on the desire for *rites of passage* (e.g., baptism, marriage and funerals) in the second session by reflecting on the

nature of such affiliate-initiated contacts and how churches can maximize their ministry to people who come to the church for those rites.

This still wasn't enough. While people were exposed to research findings and potential policy implications, there was an obvious need to go further – to explore with groups some of the tangible ways in which they might implement some of these policy implications. This third step seemed to be essential to at least get people reflecting on how they might act on the research findings and implications. Emphases such as the following emerged:

- To minister to *inactive affiliates*, groups need to use brainstorming, surveys, and cataloguing methods to find affiliates, and then arrange to have personal conversations with them to explore their interests and needs.
- To *retain children*, churches need solid ministries to children and young people.
- To *retain mobile people*, churches must systematically record members' residential moves.
- To minister to less-involved affiliates who want *rites of passage*, churches need a person who sees such requests as opportunities for ministry, and who attempts to maximize ministry, both short-term and longer-term. This can range from a short but positive contact to much more.

And so what began as a fairly detached "just the facts" one-hour lecture evolved into a morning and then into a full day of fairly intense interaction about findings, implications, and strategies. It was no accident. If institutional change is going to take place, people obviously have to go beyond merely hearing some interesting survey findings. They need to – and typically want to – know what it all means for ministry; titillating statistics, after all, at most warrant an hour or so of one's time, and only if supplemented with a good cup of coffee. Those of us who are interested in connecting such things to real life quickly grow impatient with data as such. We automatically raise the "So what?" question.

In short, this book is for people who (a) believe in God and (b) are action-oriented. There are some fascinating developments taking place in Canada today that, to my mind, can only be fully understood by someone who is open to the God factor. But those developments also can be fully appreciated only by someone who also recognizes that what is taking place calls for tangible responses, by people who aspire to participate in "the renaissance of religion in Canada."

Two more quick points as we get started. First, this book is aimed primarily at Christians, though not because of any disrespect or lack of appreciation for friends in Other Faith Groups. As we will see shortly, those who value Christian faith have a unique opportunity that may very well be the envy of people in other groups. But Christians aren't doing a particularly good job of seizing that opportunity. This book is intended to give them some help. My assumption is that, in the course of attempting to be more effective in ministering to their own, Christians will continue to work with, benefit from, and enjoy people in other faith communities – and vice versa.

Second, there has been nothing less than an explosion of congregational resources in recent years, with exports from the U.S. and Europe pouring into Canada via every possible communication form, including satellite. What this means is that Canadian church leaders these days, as in past days, invariably are looking elsewhere for solutions: particularly, of course, to Americans. Maybe they know us better than we know ourselves. Maybe we simply continue to have a national inferiority complex. Maybe Pierre Berton was right when he wrote two decades ago that when it comes to life in general, compared with the Americans, "we are not good salesmen and we are not good showmen."[1]

In any event, at minimum we need to combine the use of non-Canadian resources with a thorough and clear reading of Canadian culture and Canadian religious developments. Don Posterski and Andrew Grenville recently put things this way: "Canadians often look to America for models of effective ministry. We think they have the answers. We forget the questions may be different." The two researchers and trend watchers don't mince words: "Given the clear differences between the faith experiences of the two countries, it is clear the challenge of encouraging Canadians to integrate Church and faith demands a 'made in Canada' solution. The challenges are here. So are the solutions."[2]

What follows is "made in Canada." My hope is that it might contribute to some solutions.

The Exciting New Story About Religion in Canada

It's time for us to open our minds to the possibility that something very unexpected is occurring in Canada: organized religion is mak- ✓ ing a comeback. What's more, we may be seeing only the tip of the proverbial iceberg. Depending on the extent to which religious groups recognize and respond to what is taking place, the magnitude of that renaissance may be fairly dramatic.

The Old Story...Still Being Told

To date, the Canadian religious situation has been badly misinterpreted because it continues to be seen through the old and somewhat inflexible eyes of secularization. This age-old, taken-for-granted interpretation no longer fits the times.

Wise Men Gone Wrong

All of us have been exposed to secularization's dominant claim that religion as we have known it is in steady decline. The message has been delivered by prominent social scientists dating back to at least the late 19th and early 20th centuries – people such as Auguste Comte, Émile Durkheim, Karl Marx, and Sigmund Freud. The secularization interpretation of religion and life has been echoed in theological circles by the likes of Harvey Cox and Douglas Hall, and passed on to average Canadians by journalists, professors, and religious leaders. These days,

7

"everyone knows" organized religion has pretty much had it. A late 2003 national poll claimed that 70% of Canadians believe that new forms of spirituality are replacing traditional organized religions.[1]

However, there is very good reason to believe that "the wise men were wrong" – that people such as Marx and Freud overestimated people's ability to set aside so-called ultimate questions about the meaning of life, suffering, and death, while Durkheim badly underestimated the staying power of well-established religious groups, notably the Roman Catholic Church.[2] In recent years, Harvey Cox, who influenced the thinking of so many with his classic 1965 book, *The Secular City*, in effect left many of his long-standing secularization followers alone on a sinking ship in acknowledging that "religion seems to have gained a new lease on life," noting, "Today it is secularity, not spirituality, that may be headed for extinction." Cox admitted that "a religious renaissance of sorts is under way all over the globe.... Buddhism and Hinduism, Christianity and Judaism, Islam and Shinto, and many smaller sects are once again alive and well. Why," he wondered aloud, "were the predictors so wrong?"[3]

Retelling the Wrong Story

Unfortunately, most Canadian journalists, academics, and religious leaders are still telling the old story, adding the wrinkle that most people are interested in spirituality even if they have given up on organized religion. Little wonder that almost everyone is confused.

The pervasiveness of the passé story was readily evident in the interpretations the Canadian media gave to the latest census findings on religion, which were released in May 2003. For about a week or so, three main stories were disseminated across the country.

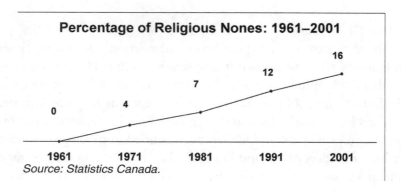

Percentage of Religious Nones: 1961–2001

0   4   7   12   16

1961   1971   1981   1991   2001

Source: Statistics Canada.

THE EXCITING NEW STORY ABOUT RELIGION IN CANADA

- The **first** was that Canadians are increasingly opting for "no religion." The assertion was based on the fact that, between 1991 and 2001, the percentage of people who indicated they have no religion increased from 12% to 16%. Accordingly, media outlets asserted that more and more Canadians are rejecting the religions of old, namely Protestantism and Catholicism. A few outlets went further. A *Toronto Star* website story, for example, carried the headline "Atheism Growing Across Canada" – even though the census findings were limited to religious identification, and had nothing at all to say about belief.

- **Second**, the nation was told that the census findings provided new evidence of the growing religious diversity of Canada. Increasing numbers of Canadians were said to be subscribing to major world faiths other than Christianity. The claim was based on census data showing that the number of Muslims, Buddhists, Hindus, and Sikhs, for example, had doubled between 1991 and 2001. In addition, many news outlets – including CBC TV's news program *The National* – played up the idea that evangelical groups had been experiencing growth over the decade. Significantly, however, *The National* was among the outlets that relied on anecdote rather than actual census findings. The proportion of people identifying with Conservative Protestant groups in fact had been found to be essentially the same as it was in 1991 – and in 1951 and in 1871, for that matter. There was and is a fascinating story associated with such evangelical stability that has important implications for the future of Other World Faiths in Canada: Conservative Protestants have been able to defy the religious assimilation odds and remain an important player on the Canadian religious scene. That story was never told.

- A **third** finding that received considerable play, particularly later in the day with the help of a Canadian Press story, was that more than 20,000 Canadians had indicated that they identify with the Jedi religion of *Star Wars* fame. Such a response was stimulated largely by the e-mail efforts of an individual from Vancouver, who in turn was following in the footsteps of similar efforts in Australia and Europe, to encourage people who objected to the religion question to offer the Jedi response. Some writers and commentators who took the 20,000-plus figure seriously suggested it was an indication that large numbers of people are turning to non-traditional expressions of religion that allow them to satisfy their increasingly individualistic spiritual quests.

These three dominant, widely circulated stories were presumed to offer sound interpretations of Canada's religious times. I suspect they were believed equally by average people who don't claim to know better and by academics and religious leaders who think they do. Unfortunately, they represented serious misreadings of what is happening on the religious front in Canada today.

Part of the problem was a methodological one. The single, simple question "What's your religion?" doesn't tell us very much about religion and tells us even less about religious commitment. It's just one lonely question in what needs to be a much more detailed conversation. We need to know what the response means to people. We also need to know if what they said yesterday is what they will say tomorrow.

But in addition, much of the problem is that the media as a whole do not know much about religious developments in Canada. I do not mean to be unfair or excessively harsh. On the positive side of religion reporting, we have a superb number of "regular beat" writers. However, for many, and probably most, journalists, the census and religion assignment was a one-day task that received little more than one day's expertise…preceded by stories that called on journalists to be instant experts on SARS, and followed by stories that expected them to be seasoned experts on mad-cow disease.

Consequently, the stories that appeared tended to reflect the journalists' stereotypes concerning evangelical churches growing, Mainline Protestant churches declining, spirituality replacing religion, and the country becoming more religiously diverse, as well as excitement about something newsy that had caught the fancy of religious consumers – this time the budding number of so-called Jedites.

The stories also reflected a predictable assumption of many journalists and other people trained in the social sciences: that Canada is experiencing relentless secularization. Sociologist Peter Berger is among those who maintain that a major reason people continue to buy into the idea of secularization is that it is propagated by people in academia, legal institutions, and the media who make the mistake of assuming their views about religion are also held by the population.[4]]

So it is that secularization interpretations of organized religion in Canada continue to appear. The Canadian edition of *Time* magazine, in its November 14, 2003, issue, featured a front cover story on religion, entitled "A Nation at Prayer." The cover included this caption:

Empty churches? They don't tell the whole story. A new poll shows that Canadians are increasingly in touch with their spiritual side.[5]

Writer Susan Catto, drawing on a summer 2003 survey of 1,202 Canadians carried out by Environics for Vision TV, informed the nation,

Canada is no longer a nation of churchgoers. Attendance at religious institutions – the old-fashioned kind, with altars and steeples – is in decline. ...[The survey] suggests that a vast majority of Canadians place a high priority on spirituality, even as significant numbers express little commitment to organized religion.... For many Canadians, spirituality has become separate from and frequently preferable to religion.[6]

The net result is that the census and *Time* stories, based primarily on a single census and a single survey respectively, and frequently interpreted through secularization glasses, have told us very little about what is actually happening to religion in Canada. Single snapshots are obviously valuable in giving us a reading at one point in time: that's why we all take photographs. But we also know that if we want to understand change, we are well advised to compare the new shots with the old ones, and keep the camera close at hand. We also are wise to play detective – to make sure we get "the story behind the story."

No Need to Remain in the Dark

Fortunately, we now have a considerable body of data on religion in Canada.

- The *federal government*, through Statistics Canada and its predecessors, has been gathering data on religious identification every 10 years since the first census of 1871. This material is invaluable. The United States, for example, does not include religion in its census. We are in the enviable position of being able to chart and analyze religious preference dating back to the country's origins.

- Besides providing the census data, since the mid–1980s Statistics Canada has conducted an annual national survey of Canadians known as the *General Social Survey* (GSS), which probes a variety of topics. These surveys are unique in that they have large sample sizes – around 15,000 – that permit detailed examinations of population characteristics.

- Most *religious groups* have been collecting a wide range of statistics on their congregations from virtually the time of their inception. Topics include membership, attendance, participation in programs such as Sunday Schools, number of congregations, number of clergy, and financial contributions. Much of this material has been published annually since the early 1970s in the *Yearbook of American and Canadian Churches*.

- Prior to about 1990, national survey material on religion was limited primarily to the work of the Gallup organization and a small number of attendance, belief, and practice items that Gallup had included in its monthly surveys; the plus was that the surveys went back as far as 1945. Since the 1990s, a growing number of *pollsters* – notably Angus Reid and its successor, Ipsos Reid, Environics, Leger and Leger, and the Strategic Counsel – have further added to our database on religion.

- I myself have been tracking religious and social trends among Canadian adults through a series of *Project Canada* national surveys every five years since 1975 and have complemented these adult surveys with *Project Teen Canada* national youth surveys in 1984, 1992, and 2000. I also included a number of religion items in a new national survey on family life that I completed in late 2003 for the Vanier Institute of the Family.[7]

We are now in a position where we can draw on fairly long-term, comprehensive findings that help to put recent census and survey data into perspective. Such analyses make it clear why the old story about religion in Canada is badly in need of an update.

The Media and *The Passion of the Christ*

Judging by most of what you read, Mel Gibson's *The Passion of the Christ* is the most dangerous, disgusting movie of all time. So why is *The Passion* doing such boffo box office? Because for millions of people across North America, *The Passion* is a deeply meaningful devotional experience.

The real rift over *The Passion* is not between the Christians and the Jews. It's between certain devout Christians and all the rest of us, especially those of little or no faith. Virtually everyone who mongers opinions in the mainstream media, including me, belongs to the latter category.

Most media folks are proudly secular types who regard openly religious people as distinctly odd. If you're gay, bi, or transgendered, we embrace you. But if your orientation is toward Jesus, you'd better keep it to yourself. We are fairly certain that born-again Christians are bigoted, not very intelligent, and possibly dangerous. This stereotype is easy to sustain because we've never actually met one.

To me, the movie was alternately riveting and revolting, moving and unwatchable. Once or twice it almost touched a chord of rapture in me, the sort of rapture that I vaguely remember feeling as a girl.

The Passion is on its way to being the biggest hit in movie history. Something's happening here, and we ought to find out what it is.

From Margaret Wente, "Passion bashin' is in fashion," *The Globe and Mail*, March 20, 2004.

The New Story: Restless Gods

Let me begin to tell the new story by drawing on those well-known words that ring down from yesteryear...

In the beginning God created the heavens and the earth...
and the Spirit of God moved over the face of the waters.

My examination of the available data leaves me with every reason to believe that in these first few years of this new century, that same Spirit of God that "moved over the face of the waters" back then is moving among Canadians and churches today. As a result, we may be seeing the early signs of a renaissance of religion in Canada.

These are days when new life is being added to old life, sometimes within religious groups but often outside of them. Things are happening that were not anticipated even a decade ago by proponents of secularization. I am among those observers who are seeing the unexpected.

Belief

Let's first look at some of the findings concerning how God seems to be touching the lives of average Canadians. There is much evidence that the God who the Apostle Paul reminded us "does not dwell in temples made with hands" has been making contact with large numbers of people across the country. Sometimes they are involved in churches – as you know well. But in many and perhaps most cases, they are also people who are not active in religious groups.

For starters, an overwhelming number of Canadians are reporting that they *believe in God*.

- At a time when only about 20% say they attend religious services just about every week, some 80% of adults and teenagers assert positive belief in God.[8]
- If that doesn't impress you, try this finding on for size: beyond sheer belief in God, no fewer than 75% of adults and 70% of teens say that they *believe in a God who cares about them personally*. Those people include one in two people who say they never attend services and one in three who say they have no religion.

Experience

But it's not just a matter that Canadians believe. Approximately one in two adults report that they themselves *have experienced God's presence*.

Experience of God Across Generations

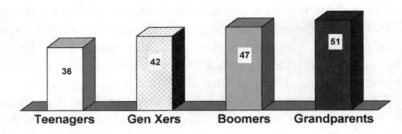

| Teenagers | Gen Xers | Boomers | Grandparents |
| 36 | 42 | 47 | 51 |

Source: Bibby, Restless Gods, 2002:150.

- What's remarkable about that level is that it has remained virtually the same since at least 1975, despite the fact that attendance at religious services dropped between 1975 and 2000 from about 30% of the population to 20%. Roughly one in three teenagers between the ages of 15 and 19 also say that they have experienced God's presence. And they haven't even hit 20 yet!

- Claims of experiencing God are highest among *Conservative Protestants* (71%), who also are typically actively involved in their churches. However, it is interesting to learn that the experience claims are also very high among *Roman Catholics in Quebec* (63%), who frequently are depicted as uninterested in religion. Particularly intriguing is the finding that no fewer than one in five people who say they have *no religion* nonetheless maintain that they personally have experienced the presence of God.

- The research also shows that when people think they have experienced God's presence, the experience has permanence. While beliefs sometimes wane as people get older, that does not tend to be the case with experience. Individuals who believe they have encountered God are inclined to retain that belief over time. Religious experience is often a profound experience with lasting effects. As United Church author Donna Sinclair notes, when people feel they have had such experiences, "there's no question but that hearts and lives are transformed."[9] While Tom Harpur is among the many who think that the pathway to truth and God is found in getting ideas straight, for many people experience is far more powerful.[10]

Prayer

But it's not just that Canadians are believing and experiencing. Very large numbers are also acknowledging that they are *talking to God* — one on one.

TABLE 1.1. **Belief, Experience, and Prayer: 1975 and 2000**

	1975	2000
BELIEF		
YES	87%	81
Yes, I definitely do	48	49
Yes, I think so	39	32
EXPERIENCE		
YES	48	47
Yes, I definitely do	22	20
Yes, I think so	26	27
PRAYER		
Daily	26	28
Weekly	10	19
Less than weekly	45	27
Never	19	26

Source: Derived from Bibby, Restless Gods, *2004:139-140,147,158.*

- Some 75% of adults pray privately at least once in a while. Moreover, one in two adults and one in three teenagers say they talk to God on a one-to-one basis at least once a week.
- As might be expected, weekly church attenders pray more than others. But one in five people who *never* attend services are praying every week or more; so are one in ten people who say they have *no religion*.

Life's Big Questions

Our research further suggests that God has also been doing a pretty good job of alerting people to the fact that there is more to life than meets the eye.[11] The so-called ultimate questions are being raised by an overwhelming majority of Canadians. About 90% say that in the course of their lifetimes they are asking the question of where we came from, how we can find lasting happiness, and what happens when we die. Even more – some 95% – acknowledge that they find themselves asking why there is suffering in the world. Sometimes life's big issues trigger the questions: a September 11th, wars, disease. But we all know that they also are tied to deeply personal experiences, such as the death of a family member or a friend, or an unexpected medical prognosis. Sometimes they are associated not with pain or stress or tragedy, but with some extremely good and happy events that cause us to marvel and wonder, such as the safe arrival of a beautiful baby. *Jms !!*

In short, people are asking the big questions. But they're not just asking. They are also believing and praying and experiencing. In the words of the old pop song, "There's a whole lot of shakin' going on." More specifically, there's a whole lot of believing and experiencing and communicating going on.[12]

And if all of this still leaves us unconvinced that God is stirring in the lives of Canadians, we need to listen as no fewer than three in four adults and two in four teens explicitly acknowledge that they have spiritual needs — needs that very often do not have their origins in exposure to churches.

Lest we be so arrogant as to think the activity of God is limited to churches, we need to hear the words of the Apostle Paul again: "God does not dwell in temples made with hands." And lest we be so naïve as to think the activity of God is dependent solely on churches, we need to read on as the Apostle adds, "Nor is God served by human hands, as though he needed anything." You see, consistent with his message, the research findings suggest God may well have grown impatient with the churches, or at least has recognized the limitations of the churches, and frequently has decided to relate directly to Canadians — to show up in Person.

In my mind, there's no doubt about it: the research points to the fact that "the Spirit of God" has been moving in the lives of large numbers of Canadians.

The New Story: Restless Churches

The research also shows that God has been moving in the lives of churches. Let's not mince words: in the post-1960s, Canada's churches probably have been something of a disappointment to God. Yet, faced with the option of dumping the established churches and trying something new, God seems to be defying critics by choosing to opt for some major renovation programs.[13] For better or worse, there is good reason to believe that God is choosing to continue to try to work through

Canada's well-established Protestant and Catholic churches. They may frustrate God, disappoint God, annoy God, and embarrass God. But to date, at least, God appears to be working to rejuvenate them.

There are at least **four empirical signs** that God is stirring in the established churches, bringing about new life.

Teenagers

In recent years there has been an unexpected increase in the proportion of teenagers who are actively involved. Our national surveys of 15- to 19-year-olds show that, in 1984, 23% were attending services on a regular weekly basis. That figure dropped to 18% in 1992. Had you asked me in early 2000 what I thought the new national survey that year would find with respect to attendance, I would have estimated that the weekly level would have slipped to around 13%. To my surprise, the figure came in at 22% – bouncing back to essentially the level of the mid-'80s. It was not what the proponents of ongoing, linear secularization had expected.[14]

TABLE 1.2. **Service Attendance of Teens by Group: 1984–2000**			
	1984	1992	2000
NATIONALLY	23%	18	22
Protestant	26	30	48
Conservative	51	61	70
Mainline	17	16	23
Anglican	*13*	*14*	*16*
United	*17*	*13*	*17*
Roman Catholic	28	21	21
Outside Quebec	37	27	31
Quebec	16	11	7
Other Faiths	13	15	21
None	3	2	3

Source: Derived from Bibby, Restless Gods, *2004:88.*

Young Adults

In the last decade or so there also have been signs of new interest among young adults. For the first time since the 1960s, Protestants have seen an increase in recent years in the proportion of adults under the age of 35 who are attending services weekly. Roman Catholics, after experiencing a significant drop-off in young-adult attendance in the 1970s and 1980s, have seen attendance levels stabilize – albeit at a low level in Quebec.

TABLE 1.3. Attendance Levels of Protestant and Catholic 18- to-34-Year-Olds: 1975–2000

	1975 & 1980	1990	2000
Protestant	16%	20	26
Roman Catholic	22	16	12
Outside Quebec	29	20	18
Quebec	19	7	5

Sources: 1975 & 1980: Bibby, Project Canada Survey Series; 1990 & 2000: Statistics Canada, General Social Survey (1990) and Survey of Giving, Volunteering, and Participating (2000).

Congregational Reports

Third, people in the pews are reporting that growing congregations are fairly common across the country. Asked pointedly in 2000 about recent growth patterns in their local congregations and parishes, one in three Canadians who are active in their churches indicated that their groups have been growing. Another one in three said they have stayed about the same. Contrary to widespread belief, only one in three said that their groups have been decreasing in size. Some might protest that churches in smaller towns and rural areas are an exception: they are dying. Actually, the only notable variation by community size to "the one-third, one-third, one-third pattern" is the somewhat greater likelihood of people living in smaller areas to say their church sizes have been staying about the same. Overall, such reports hardly warrant the common gloom and doom generalizations about the demise of the churches.

	GROWING	STAYING SAME	DECLINING	TOTALS
NATIONALLY	36%	32	32	100
Protestants	47	31	22	100
Conservative	59	28	13	100
Mainline	32	36	32	100
Roman Catholics	24	33	43	100
Outside Quebec	33	35	32	100
Quebec	11	32	57	100

TABLE 1.4. **Congregational and Parish Numerical Trends**
"If you attend religious services once a month or more: in recent years, has your group been…"

Source: Bibby, Restless Gods, *2004:79.*

To date the resurgence of organized religion in Canada has been led by *Conservative Protestant*, evangelical denominations such as Baptists, Pentecostals, Mennonites, the Christian and Missionary Alliance, and a growing number of independent charismatic congregations. These groups are highly committed to evangelism, a key to understanding the vitality and intensity that so often is found among their leaders and their churches. However, there also are important signs of new life among *Roman Catholics outside Quebec*, as well as *Mainline Protestants:* United, Anglican, Lutheran, and Presbyterian churches.[15] Qualitative research carried out for the Anglican Church of Canada in 2002 by Environics, for example, included the following observation:

> No matter how diverse the concerns and fears expressed…all across Canada, [Anglicans] reported signs of joy: new music and new musical skills have become part of some churches for the first time; among evangelical churches there are growing populations, including young families; among some mainstream churches there is a sense of commitment to participate in programs for social justice; among some Church members there is a commitment to seeking a path toward spiritual learning.[16]

What typically characterizes growing congregations is their strong emphasis on ministry to children, young people, and young adults, and their effort to address the spiritual, personal, and relational needs of people of all ages. Catholics and Mainline Protestants have followed the lead of Conservative Protestants in giving explicit renewed emphasis to youth ministry, good worship, spirituality, Bible studies, and prayer – while continuing to place importance on social and justice issues.[17] Not surprisingly, many such churches are either located in new residential areas or are accessing new areas in the course of redefining themselves as regional versus neighbourhood churches.[18]

Consequently, the new interest of younger adults and teenagers is no accident. In the late 1980s, Roman Catholics, for example – perhaps spurred on by Pope John Paul II's declaration that "youth are the hope of the Church" – accelerated their efforts to relate more effectively to children, teens, and young adults, complete with full-time and part-time youth ministry specialists.[19] The same has been increasingly true of Mainline Protestants.[20] In the case of teenagers, groups have been working hard to develop ministry environments that are sensitive to the premier teen values of friendship and freedom, their enjoyment of music and other media, and their receptivity to spirituality.

TABLE 1.5. **Some Ministry Priorities of Canadian Anglicans**
"It is important to belong to a church that…"

Reaches out to youth	90%
Helps one achieve spiritual growth	79
Can attract new members	76
Responds to the needs of the poor	71
Reaches out to Aboriginal communities	46
Pressures govts to spend more on social programs	43
Welcomes gays and lesbians	33

Source: Environics September 2002 poll of 1,062 Anglican members, The General Synod of the Anglican Church of Canada, 2004:AD2.

Recent Polls

⌐A fourth indicator of resurgence? The results of all this church activity are beginning to show up in national attendance figures. A spring 2002 national survey conducted by Allan Gregg's Strategic Counsel claimed that weekly church attendance could be as high as 30% of the population.[21] My own latest national poll, conducted for the Vanier Institute of the Family and completed in August of 2003, found that 26% of Canadian adults say they are attending services approximately once a week. The poll I referred to earlier that was also completed around the same time for Vision TV and published in *Time* magazine pegged the weekly attendance figure at a very similar 27%.[22] These are the highest levels reported by Canadians since around 1985. Needless to say, they hardly warrant the conclusion that the country is characterized by "empty churches." ⌐

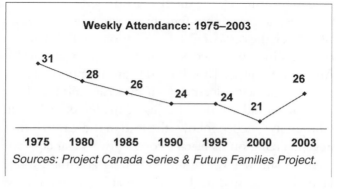

Weekly Attendance: 1975–2003

31 28 26 24 24 21 26

1975 1980 1985 1990 1995 2000 2003

Sources: Project Canada Series & Future Families Project.

Think of it: one in four Canadian adults in services on any given weekend…some five million people – plus lots of kids. There is no other group activity in Canada that begins to compare with such a level of involvement. Try on pro sports, for example: total church service attendance on an average weekend surpasses a typical Grey Cup or Super Bowl television audience in Canada. It's more than the total number of fans our six Canadian NHL teams combined draw in an entire season (about 750,000 x 6) – with a fraction of the marketing, publicity and corporate support. And what's more, the service average doesn't include "the occasional fans." Still further, remember that the latest evidence indicates the "fan base" of religious groups is growing.

The Quebec Exception

The asterisk on such signs of a religious renaissance currently is attached to Quebec. One prominent Ottawa journalist recently suggested to me that Quebec is "a religious wasteland." For years, many evangelical groups have seen Quebec as "a ripe mission field." Both views are badly out of touch with reality.

Quebec continues to be thoroughly Catholic. If a renaissance occurs, it will be a Catholic renaissance. But it's not as if the Church has to start from scratch. Some 80% of Quebec Catholics acknowledge that they have spiritual needs, and a similar proportion say they believe in a God who cares about them personally. They don't stop with abstract belief: 81% report that they pray privately, 51% at least once a week. Moreover, the 63% of Quebec Catholics who maintain they have experienced God's presence is second only to evangelical Protestants (71%). And as we will see shortly, significant numbers indicate they are receptive to greater involvement – if they can find it to be worthwhile.

It would seem to be just a matter of time before the Catholic Church in Quebec follows the lead of the Church in the rest of Canada in capitalizing on its blatant competitive advantage, and responds to the interests and needs that are so readily apparent. Indeed, historian Jean Hamelin suggested in the 1980s that a genuine renewal was beginning to take place within the Quebec Catholic Church. He went so far as to suggest that "the noise of the things that are dying still drown out the voice of the things that are coming to birth."[23] However, the Church in Quebec may well need a bit of help from some like-minded people in some other religious families. This important issue is one we will return to as we explore some radical possibilities in Chapter 3.

Canadian Ministry – Willow Creek–Style

These days, evangelicals in particular are tapping into what seems like an explosion of ministry resources. Among the most prominent are those emanating from the independent Willow Creek Community Church in South Barrington, Illinois, near Chicago, whose senior pastor is Bill Hybels. "Willow Creek Canada" works through what is known as The Leadership Centre, located near Kelowna, British Columbia.

Churches are encouraged to become Canadian members of the Willow Creek Association Canada. Heading into 2004, "WCAC" claimed to have close to 800 members from "more than 50 denominations in 250 cities across Canada, from Victoria in the west to Halifax in the east and as far north as Yellowknife." Member churches are called upon to become what is referred to as "Prevailing Churches." Such churches are portrayed as building devotion, connecting lives, and transforming communities. Churches are offered an extremely wide range of resources, including curriculum materials for children ("Promiseland"), youth and student ministry, worship, music, drama, small groups, preaching, Bible study, stewardship, evangelism, personal growth, the Natural Church Development congregational evaluation tool – even the Alpha Program. In addition to books and other written materials, most of these highly diverse offerings are available on or accompanied by VHS, DVD, and PowerPoint.

Still further, national "Prevailing Church Conferences" that variously focus on ministry generally, leadership, student ministry, children's ministry, small groups, and evangelism are held in numerous sites across Canada each year. They feature Willow Creek Community Church and Canadians from some leading WCAC churches. For example, four conferences were held in 2003 and five were scheduled for 2004, with the 2004 schedule including "The Leadership Summit" beamed by satellite to 12 different Canadian locations. Promotional materials encourage people to "Bring a team of pastors, staff, and volunteers for a life-changing, church-changing event you'll never forget!" Membership and conference participation is "for churches, ministries, and leaders who hold to an historic, orthodox understanding of biblical Christianity."

This is big: potentially an American-based ministry that is transcending denominational boundaries in impacting churches that are primarily part of Canada's Conservative Protestant sector. It has critically important implications for the way those churches will attempt to carry out ministry and share – or fail to share – in Canada's emerging religious renaissance.

Primary Information Source: Leadership on the Edge, *The Leadership Centre Willow Creek Canada, Winfield, BC, Issue 23, Fall 2003.*

Premature Obituaries

[In the post-1960s, lots of people gave up on the churches. However, these kinds of research findings suggest that God didn't give up on Canada's churches. On the contrary, there is reason to believe that God is stirring in the churches – shaking them up even as God has been stirring in the lives of Canadians.

Then again, perhaps such divine faith in the established churches should not be all that surprising. Long-standing organizations do not readily disappear. Major banks and universities and long-established corporations change with the times and remain with us. Why should well-established religious groups be any different? Why, therefore, were we so quick to give up on the churches?

After all, Anglicanism and the United Church, Presbyterianism and Lutheranism, along with Roman Catholicism in Quebec, are not exactly fly-by-night operations. They have long histories and recuperative powers. They don't just roll over and die. History tells us that, rather than expecting them to go into receivership in troubled times, we would be wise to expect them to retreat, retrench, revamp, and resurface.[24] Many are part of durable national and multinational corporations with headquarters in places such as Toronto, Rome, and Canterbury. Some have substantial roots and resources in the United States. In discussing the potential of the Catholic Church, for example, to have impact not only in Canada but worldwide, Michael Higgins and Douglas Letson remind us that "The Catholic Church is a spiritual communion with over 1 billion members, a Church large enough to make a difference in the world."[25]

These kinds of prominent Canadian religious groups also have brand-name credibility and thousands and thousands of affiliates who are extremely slow to turn elsewhere. I can't stress enough that those people who identify with the existing religious groups are *customers with a difference*: many have significant psychological and emotional ties to the well-established groups that run through their grandparents and parents and other family members and friends. They don't bounce freely from group to group, like customers bouncing from one mall and one store to another.

Ironically, it seems that precisely when long-established groups reach low points, people who are particularly committed to turning things around show up, and contribute to new signs of life.[26] Unexpected things happen. Just recently, for example, priest and trend-watcher Andrew Greeley has noted that, for better or worse, there is evidence that a generation of conservative young priests is on the rise in the U.S. – priests who "seem in many ways intent on restoring the pre-Vatican II Church."[27] Maybe they will become more liberal as they get older. Maybe they won't. But they do appear to be highly committed and may well have an impact that could extend to Canada.

Consequently, if major companies without the loyal customer advantage of large, well-established religious groups can frequently turn themselves around, it would be foolish to bet against the potential for revitalization among Canada's long-standing religious groups. If (a) the people are still out there and (b) the groups are still there, it makes good sense to assume that it will only be a matter of time before they experience rejuvenation.

And if, beyond these organizational realities, God decides to work with and through the existing churches rather than dump them, who knows what's possible? So far it would seem that restoration continues to be the Divine preference. There's some impressive evidence for this apparent choice that we want to look at next.

2

Getting
the Facts Straight

If the confusion about the state of religion in Canada were limited only to journalists, that would be unfortunate but not necessarily a critical problem for religious groups. What is much more serious about the confusion is that it is also widespread among religious leaders and active laity. A misreading of the times is leading to poorly informed policies that, in turn, have led to programs and activities that have made little impact on people outside the country's churches. Peter Berger's widely cited observation a number of decades ago still applies: "Christian commitment involves commitment to clear perception."[1] It's also essential to combine that perception with clarity about what religious groups are doing. In the words of Higgins and Letson, "The need for Catholics and others to try and understand what goes on in the Church is inexhaustible."[2] It's time we got beyond seeing through a glass darkly. This takes us back to the three main stories surrounding the 2003 release of our latest census findings on religion.

Most People Aren't Dropping Out

The growth in the proportion of Canadians who say they have "no religion" is widely seen as evidence of growing disenchantment with religious groups. This is a precarious assumption.

The Growing Number of "Religious Nones"

The Globe and Mail was among the news outlets that played up the increase in the number of people who said they have no religion, noting the figure "was up by 43.9 per cent between 1991 and 2001." Writer Gloria Galloway went on to say that, in contrast with groups such as Muslims, major Protestant churches "that spawned the old generation of Canada's power elite are on the wane." She added, "It seems the biggest blow to the Protestant churches was – and continues to be – a drift away from organized religion." Roman Catholics, she suggested, were able to increase their ranks "as a result of immigration from countries like the Philippines where that faith is still strong."[3]

There's no doubt about it: the proportion of Canadians who say "nothing" when asked, "What is your religion?" has been on the rise. The 2001 census pegged the figure of "Religious Nones" (as they are known to social scientists) at 16%, versus 12% in 1991. The size of the latest figure is even more impressive when compared with the 4% level of 1971 – the first year that the census-takers literally took "no" for an answer – and 7% in 1981.

On the surface, those findings suggest that increasing numbers of Canadians are rejecting religion. You know some; so do I. They're out there. I'm reminded of an articulate teenager who appeared with me on an Edmonton phone-in show in the early 1990s. Asked by veteran host Ron Collister if she was religious, she smiled pleasantly and responded, "No – I'm from a religion-free home." What the findings show is that a growing number of people say they have "no religion" *at some point* in their lives. What typically is not understood, however, is that the claim is not usually permanent. That's why we need to keep some film in the research camera.

"No Religion" and Life Stage

As census findings continue to show, people who say they have "no religion" are disproportionately young: 75% are under 45, 40% are under 25. In fact, one in four are actually children under 15 whose parents have reported their "no religion" status for them.

I have charted "Religious Nones" through my Project Canada national surveys for some time now. About one in three come from homes where their parents also have no religion. However, one in three come from Catholic homes and most of the remaining one in three from Protestant homes, primarily United Church and Anglican. Within five years, about one in three of these "nothings" become "something"; within ten years, the figure increases to about two in three.

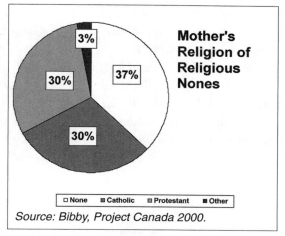

Mother's Religion of Religious Nones

3% · 37% · 30% · 30%

□ None ▪ Catholic ▪ Protestant ▪ Other

Source: Bibby, Project Canada 2000.

As these predominantly younger people get older, marry, and have children, they typically turn to religious groups for pivotal rites of passage. When they do, their choices, of course, are not random: most turn to the identification groups of their parents. When subsequently asked, "What is your religion," guess what? They no longer are "nothing."

Today's 15- to 19-year-olds illustrate the pattern well. My Project Teen Canada national survey of some 3,500 teenagers in late 2000 found that 24% indicated they had no religion. However, when asked if they anticipated turning to religious groups in the future for a marriage ceremony, 79% of these same "no religion" teens said "yes"; the overall national level was 89%.

In the midst of going from "something" to "nothing" and back to "something," Religious Nones most certainly are not necessarily atheists: 40% of adults and 35% of teenagers who report having no religion not only say they believe in God, they say they believe in a God who cares about them. There's more: some 35% of adults and 30% of teens in this category acknowledge that they pray privately. For the record, about one in three adult and teenage Nones also show up for a worship service at least once in awhile. ⌐

"Less than Weekly" Does Not Equal "Dropout"

This last point is worth amplifying. When observers are looking at attendance trends, they invariably look at weekly attendance and assume that if people are not attending on a regular weekly basis, they have dropped out. But to the extent that we pollsters give respondents a wide range of response choices when we ask the attendance question, what we find is that only about 20% of Canadians actually say that they "never" attend services. What's more, that 20% core has remained remarkably stable since at least the mid-1970s.

That means that the highly publicized attendance decline of the post-1960s has primarily taken the form of people attending less often, rather than not attending at all. Most of that taken-for-granted talk about people "dropping out" and "going back to church" is groundless.

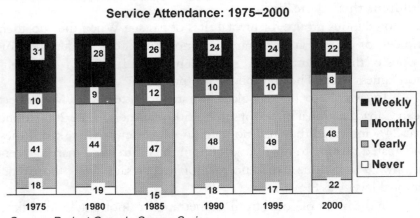

Source: Project Canada Survey Series.

Some fast facts:
- Few drop out; few go back.
- Most continue to identify with groups and attend occasionally; they don't drop out – they drop in.
- To the extent that groups experience numerical declines, those declines reflect death rather than defection: active members die and are not replaced by new active members.

I've been saying for years that, ironically, rather than readily losing people, the major religious groups in reality have extreme difficulty losing them.[4] Even when churches triumphantly pare the names of inactive people from their church lists and proclaim them to be "dead wood," such apparent recalcitrants go on thinking that they are Baptists, Anglicans, Lutherans, Presbyterians, United Church, and so on. You will notice that I didn't include "Roman Catholics" in that list. That's because the tendency to equate the lack of involvement with religious defection tends to be a misreading that is far more common among Protestants than Catholics. If people are baptized Catholic, they are Catholics until they officially recant...and perhaps even after they do! But not to be involved in a Protestant church is tantamount to apostasy, and seemingly calls for ostracism regardless of how loudly the outcast protests. Here Protestants have chosen to let theology override social and psychological reality.

So it is that in my 1985 examination of Anglicans in the Toronto Diocese, I was somewhat shocked to find that no less than 80% of the people in the study who described themselves as "inactive" Anglicans nonetheless said that being an Anglican is important to them. The archbishop at the time, Lewis Garnsworthy, summed up the situation with these widely cited words: "It's not that they're leaving – it's just that they're not coming." In the late 1970s, singer Bonnie Tyler had a hit song entitled "It's a Heartache." Included on the album with that hit was a melodramatic love song that included the poignant words "Love songs last longer than lovers ever do." A slight edit of that line sums up the religious reality that so many people often miss: "Religious identification lasts longer than involvement ever does."

A fair reading of the latest census data on religion is that 84% of Canadians continue to identify with religious groups, despite apparent secularization and the availability of a growing number of options. These additional Project Canada trend findings suggest that they soon will be joined by many "temporary Nones" who are currently part of the remaining 16%.

By the way, the "no religion" figure for the U.S. as of 2001 was 14%, up from 8% in 1990. The media "down there" likewise assumed "more people than ever are opting out." Maybe they can learn something from us.[5]

Most People Aren't Switching

A second series of stories circulated by the media on the heels of the census release focused on the options being selected by people who are disenchanted with the established groups.

Religious Upgrading

As mentioned earlier, the evening of the religion release, *The National* on CBC TV informed us that growing numbers of Canadians are turning to evangelical Protestant groups, and used Calgary as an illustration. Other news outlets such as Canadian Press (CP) played up the 20,000 people who declared themselves to be followers of Jedi, while acknowledging that "the Jedi membership drive" was actually a gag aimed at thumbing noses at the government for asking the question about one's religion. But CP went on to cite experts who argue that young people who are frustrated with organized religions are experimenting with spirituality.[6] Additional stories looked at the inroads of smaller and newer groups. The assumption, of course, was that many Canadians are in effect switching groups.

It's not a new thesis. The decline in regular service attendance since the 1960s has led many observers to argue that large numbers of people are playing what American sociologist Andrew Greeley once referred to as "religious musical chairs";[7] today another metaphor might be "upgrading." A decade ago, my friend and colleague Don Posterski was among those who argued that "denominational walls are tumbling down."[8] The pervasiveness of the idea that people these days shop for churches like they shop for furniture was reinforced when a U.S. Nazarene author, Carmen Renee Berry, came out with a book in 2003 entitled *The Unauthorized Guide to Choosing a Church*.[9]

In the past few years, American author Wade Clark Roof (*Spiritual Marketplace*) and Carleton University's Peter Emberley (*Divine Hunger*) have maintained that many people not only are variously moving from one religious group to another, but frequently are opting for less-structured settings in the course of engaging in highly personal and groupless spiritual quests.[10] In the words of Mark McGowan, the principal of Toronto's St. Michael's College, "People have moved away, not from faith or spirituality, but from institutionalized religion. They have taken what they want from a variety of different faith perspectives and made it personal."[11] I constantly run into clergy who claim that people almost randomly show up in their churches, either disenchanted with other groups or with "no" religious background. Based on conversations with United Church ministers, freelance writer Melissa Walker recently wrote:

> Newcomers of every stripe seek spiritual nurture wherever they can find it; and it so happens that often it's in the United Church. In fact, in conversations with clergy from 20 successful (and usually growing) United Church congregations across Canada, this is a recurring theme: many newcomers have no United Church background. Instead, they come from a variety of faith backgrounds, including Roman Catholic, Baptist and Presbyterian. Or they arrive with no church background at all. In some churches, the number of ethnic members, often recent converts, is rising.[12]

In sum, such thinking suggests that Canadians are frequently religious free agents who not only church-shop but also browse spiritual marketplaces and meaning malls, resolving their religious and spiritual needs by making consumer-like choices based primarily on their personal tastes and whims. Presumably they upgrade their religious and spiritual preferences just about as easily as they upgrade their computers and software. What drives the choices is "what works best."

Religion's Powerful Social and Cultural Foundation

As I emphasized in *Restless Gods*, sociologically speaking, such a switching thesis doesn't makes much sense.[13] If religion were simply a product, individuals would indeed shop for religions like they shop for computers. If religion simply consisted of ideas, we could abandon them as easily as we say goodbye to our beliefs in Santa and the Easter bunny and the tooth fairy. But, as we all know well, religion is far more than a product or an idea. Our experiences in religious groups are replete with cultures and memories that typically are grounded in our family and important life-stages: birth, childhood, adulthood, marriage, and death.

Moreover, we get used to worshipping in certain ways and, frankly, often feel awkward in settings that are very different from our own. Most Catholics don't exactly feel immediately at ease in a Baptist service. Baptists typically feel more than a little lost and uncomfortable in a Catholic service. Why? Well, for starters, the sanctuaries look different, the hymns aren't the same, the worship styles are different, and the two groups are doing very different things with water.

As it is with Catholics and Baptists, so it is with other religious groups. What is normal in one setting is downright different in another; what is emotionally moving in one church leaves people untouched in another. It's all about religious culture. Want a quick reality check? Just think of how you have felt when you sat in on weddings and funerals in some of those churches that are different from yours....

And then there's that loyalty I referred to earlier that makes people "customers with a difference" – loyalty that is sometimes blatant, sometimes latent, sometimes rational, sometimes irrational. One reacts to a joke about the pope...or a putdown of evangelicals...or a knock against the United Church. In the face of anger or discontent, for most, switching is not an option. In a recent article in *Catholic New Times*, New Brunswick priest Father Jeff Doucette decries the way Catholics are discouraged from speaking up about issues that seem "unjust within our church." He writes, "I strongly believe that if priests do not begin to find the courage and begin to voice what is in their hearts, our church will never change." He concludes, "Why have I not removed my stole and walked away? It is because I have a responsibility as a baptized member of our church to stay and be part of the solution. I hope using my voice in a loving, serving and just way will encourage other priests and lay people to find their voice and use it."[14] In like manner, Rev. Rudy Plug, a disenchanted United Church minister, rhetorically asks, "Tell me again why we should stay in the United Church of Canada? When is enough enough?" His answer: "In short, the UCC needs people like you and me. If everyone decided to jump ship, the ship would run aground or sink."[15]

A journalist with a denominational newspaper who took a summer course with me at McMaster Divinity College recently described her deep-seated sense of loyalty to her group this way:

Religious loyalties seem to be bred in the bone. What was learned and experienced seems to stick with people for life, and connects us with those who have gone before us. I recall going to a church that my grandmother, great-grandmother, and great-great-grandmother had attended. The mystery of that experience blew me away. I could almost hear them, like that "cloud of witnesses" you read about in Scripture, cheering me on from the sidelines of that empty church.

Given the facts of religious culture and religious family history, basic sociology tells us that there is little reason to expect that large amounts of switching will take place. Most people will be reluctant to wander very far from their religious homes. If they feel such an inclination, they typically will have a parent or partner or friend who will discourage them from doing so.

What the Research Shows

Our research findings spanning the last three decades support such a hunch. The vast majority of Canadians are reluctant to try just any supplier. Most stick with the choices of their parents and grandparents. For example, some 90% of Catholics in Quebec and 80% of Catholics elsewhere identify with the religion of their mothers. Protestants not only tend to stay within the Protestant category but also are inclined to remain within the Mainline and Conservative "religious families," regardless of how much internal denominational switching (such as United to Anglican, Mennonite to Baptist) may go on. To the extent that people "switch," they tend to move into the "no religion" category – and guess where many of them will eventually end up….

TABLE 2.1. **Extent and Nature of Intergenerational Switching: 2000**

Mother's Religion	RC	MLProt	CProt	Other	None	Totals
RCs: Quebec	**89**%	<1	<1	1	9	100
RCs: Outside Quebec	**80**	4	1	3	12	100
Mainline Protestants	6	**78**	4	3	9	100
Conservative Protestants	<1	18	**71**	<1	11	100
Other Faiths	7	4	<1	**71**	18	100
Nones	11	11	5	<1	**74**	100

RESPONDENT'S RELIGION

Source: Bibby, Restless Gods, 2004:42.

TABLE 2.2. Openness to Switching Traditions
% Indicating "No"

	NAT	RCs Out Q	RCs Quebec	ML Prots	Cons Prots	Other Faiths
Nationally	83%	87	97	75	81	61
Weeklys	92	93	98	86	87	★★
<Weekly	80	83	97	72	72	★★

Source: Drawn from Bibby, Restless Gods, 2004:44.

Moreover, in 2000 we asked Canadians explicitly if they are open to switching to another religious tradition. Some 92% of those attending services every week indicated that they are not open to switching; no surprise there. But among those who attend monthly or less, 80% also said no. In Quebec, the "not interested" figure for weekly attending Catholics was 98%; for Catholics who attend less often the figure was 97%! So much for the idea that Quebec – and for that matter, most of the rest of the country – is an open "religious market," ripe for inroads by non-Catholic groups.

If People Switched, Who Grew?

Let's face it – if people had actually "dropped out" of Canada's dominant religious groups in the post-1950s and were on the lookout for new ones, some of the alternative "religious companies" should have experienced significant growth. After all, weekly attendance dropped from some 50% to 20%.

Yet, census data spanning 1951 through 2001 show that groups such as Jehovah's Witnesses (.2% – .6%), Latter-Day Saints (.2% – .3%), and Unitarians (.1% – .1%) experienced negligible growth relative to the population. The latest census, for example, has found that our country of some 30 million people now includes a whopping 1,525 individuals who identify with the highly publicized New Age movement, another 1,525 with Scientology, and a further 850 who see their religion as Satanist. Incidentally, we also have 2,100 explicit humanists, which will be seen by some as "phenomenal growth" since the total represents a 68% increase from 1991.

It may be that, in the future, such groups will expand beyond the fringes of Canadian life, and as such they are certainly worth watching. But currently they are on the sidelines, as they and other would-be competitors have been throughout our country's history.

TABLE 2.3. **Sizes of Select Smaller Religious Groups: 2001**

Jehovah's Witnesses	154,750
Latter-Day Saints	101,805
Aboriginal Spirituality	29,820
Pagan	21,085
Baha'i	18,020
Unitarian	17,480
Spiritualist	3,295
New Age	1,525
Scientology	1,525
Rastafarian	1,135
Satanist	850

Source: Statistics Canada, 2001 Census.

What About Evangelicals?

You may find yourself asking a question that undoubtedly is on the minds of a number of readers: what about evangelical Protestants? They certainly seem to be growing. Where are all their people coming from?

It's an important question with an important answer. I mentioned earlier that the first census, in 1871, found that approximately 8% of Canadians identified with Conservative Protestant groups. In 1951 the figure remained at about 8%. As of the 2001 census, the percentage is still around 8%. As we have just seen, evangelical denominations seem to have limited success in recruiting people who identify with other traditions. However, to be able to hold on to 8% of the population since Canada came into being, versus be assimilated, is a remarkable achievement. Such success is the envy of every small religious group in the country – and of more than a few larger ones as well.

The Top 10 Evangelical Churches in Canada
By Average Weekly Attendance

1. Springs of Living Water	Independent	Winnipeg	9,000
2. Centre Street Church	Evangelical Miss. Church	Calgary	3,711
3. The Peoples' Church	Independent	Toronto	2,910
4. Agincourt Pentecostal Church	PAOC	Scarborough	2,800
5. Northview Community Church	Mennonite Brethren	Abbotsford	2,701
6. Trinity Baptist Church	North American Baptist	Kelowna	2,500
7. Christian Life Assembly	PAOC	Langley	2,345
8. Beulah Alliance	Christian & Miss. Alliance	Edmonton	2,078
9. Kennedy Road Tabernacle	PAOC	Brampton	2,000
10. Sherwood Park Alliance	Christian & Miss. Alliance	Sherwood Park	1,995

Source: Christian Week, *Spring 2003:5. There might be some larger; the publication says these are "10 of the largest."*

The key to evangelicals' proportional stability – and numerical growth, of course, with the increase in the size of the national population – appears to lie in their ability to hold on to their children and geographically mobile members. Such retention, in turn, seems clearly related to such features as explicit ministries to youth and families, vitality and enthusiasm that result in inviting environments (their young people not only participate but actually enjoy it!), and strong emphases on spirituality and relationships. As an executive for the more liberally minded National Council of Churches, Dean Kelley, noted three decades ago in a classic work aimed at helping Mainliners learn from evangelicals, Conservative Protestants also demand a lot of their members, a feature that sociologist Rodney Stark maintains is essential to a religious group's viability.[16]

But research on evangelical growth indicates that, despite their best intentions and efforts, such groups have limited success in reaching people outside their boundaries. My examination of the growth patterns of 20 Calgary evangelical churches between 1966 and 2000, for example, has found that about 70% of the new additions during that 40-year period were geographically mobile evangelicals, 15% were their children, and only about 15% were people from outside the so-called evangelical community. To the extent that the evangelism of outsiders took place, the key factors were not primarily things like services, activities, or programs. The two key variables were *friendship* and *marriage* – or, in one word, relationships.

TABLE 2.4. **Sources of New Members in Conservative Protestant Churches: 1966–2000**

Period	Reaffiliation	Birth	Proselytism	Totals
1996–00	69%	14	17	100
1986–90	72	13	15	100
1976–80	70	17	13	100
1966–70	72	19	9	100

Source: Bibby, Circulation of the Saints Study, 2003.

The lesson to be learned from the evangelical experience is an important one: if a congregation in any religious group wants to grow, the key is focusing on members' children and people on the move geographically. If a church wants to reach outsiders, that's a different and difficult story. It calls for highly conscious and well-thought-out strategies – a topic I return to in Chapter 5.

In sum, the prevalence of switching has been grossly exaggerated. We shouldn't expect a lot of it, and we don't see a lot of it. Of course, some switching between religious families takes place; no one's denying that. And when it does, some possible consequences are well worth noting – such as the impact of former evangelical leaders such as Don Posterski (formerly Nazarene), Maxine Hancock (Alliance), and Ronald Kydd (formerly Pentecostal) on Anglicans, and William "Bud" Phillips (formerly Baptist) on Mainliners as principal of the Vancouver School of Theology. It is also worth reflecting on the impact of the movement of people from other families into the Conservative Protestant family, such as Jewish-raised Albert Runge, who served as the pastor of one of the largest Alliance churches in Canada, and ... and ... and ... [I just used one of my three lifelines to call evangelical historical guru John Stackhouse to help me finish the sentence, and he, too, was lost for names, which – I guess – further documents my argument about limited switching occurring between families]. Lest you think I forgot, illustrations of high-level leaders who switched to and from Roman Catholicism are invited.

Christianity is Still Dominant

The third census finding that received considerable attention from journalists was the increase in the number of Canadians who identify with major world religions other than Christianity. As of 2001, there were 580,000 people subscribing to Islam, more than double the 253,000 figure in 1991. Over that decade, Buddhist affiliates rose from 163,000 to 300,000, Hindus from 157,000 to 297,000, and Sikhs from 147,000 to 278,000. A widely distributed Canadian Press story summed up the prevalent media interpretation of such developments: "The increase in the proportion of Canadians with no religion as well as the substantial increases in religions such as Hindu, Sikh and Buddhism illustrate Canada's growing diversity."[17]

The Reality of Religious Assimilation

It is premature, however, to assume that these major world faiths are making or will make a major dent in the Catholic and Protestant religious monopoly in this country. Measured as percentages of the total national population, the figures are still very small: 2% for Muslims, 1% each for Buddhists, Hindus, and Sikhs. A cause for pause is that the first Canadian census in 1871 found that about 2% of Canadians identified with faiths other than Christianity, including Judaism. As of 1991 the figure had reached just 4%. The 2001 census figure is only 6%. It may not go much higher.

TABLE 2.5. **Religious Identification of Canadians, 1871–2001**

Identification	1871	1901	1931	1961	1991	2001
Roman Catholic	42%	42	41	47	46	44
Protestant	56	56	54	49	36	32
Eastern Orthodox	<1	<1	1	1	2	2
Other Faiths	2	2	3	2	4	6
No Religion	<1	<1	<1	<1	12	16

Source: Derived from Statistics Canada census data.

Very significantly, the census release pointed out that much of the recent growth in a variety of world faiths has been due to immigration and birth, not the conversion of additional Canadians. Over the long haul, if groups such as Muslims and Buddhists are to continue to keep up with, let alone exceed, population growth, it is critically important that they be able to do what every viable religious group has to do: retain their children. The problem they face is one that is well known to all smaller religious groups, ranging from Jews through Baptists: how to avoid religious assimilation. Their daughters and sons have small pools of only 1–2% of the youth population to draw from when it comes to marital choices; compare that to young Catholics, for example, who can select partners from just under 50% of the national population – a figure that soars to close to 90% in Quebec.

Socializing and Marriage

So it is that we have found in our Project Teen Canada survey that by the time young people who were raised in Buddhist, Hindu, Muslim, or Sikh homes reach their late teens, some 15% are saying that they have no religious preference, and around 5% see themselves as Protestants or Catholics. Reflecting the lack of reciprocity in the religious assimilation process, less than 1% of teenagers with a Protestant or Catholic parent identify with any of those four major Other Faith traditions.

The problem is particularly acute when religious intermarriage occurs. Census data for 1991, for example, show that when Canadians who identify with Other World Faiths marry a Protestant, a Catholic, a Jew, or even a "Religious None," the dominant tendency is for the children to be raised in the religion (or no religion) of the partner.

TABLE 2.6. **Identification of Children and Identification of Mothers and Fathers**

RELIGION OF			RELIGION OF CHILDREN				
Mother	*Father*	*No. of Couples*	*Catholic*	*Prot*	*Other Faiths*	*No Religion*	*Totals*
Catholic	Other Faiths	7,600	**58**	1	21	20	100
Other Faiths	Catholic	3,195	**58**	4	12	26	100
Protestant	Other Faiths	5,735	1	**45**	26	28	100
Other Faiths	Protestant	3,220	2	**43**	26	29	100
Other Faiths	No Religion	4,415	3	5	22	**70**	100

Source: Adapted from Bibby, 2001:83. Data: Statistics Canada, 1991 census.

The 2001 growth figures for major global religions signal the potential for increased religious diversity. There's no doubt that committed immigrants have brought much energy and new resources to the Canadian religious "market." But until such groups achieve "critical size masses" that contribute to their being able to retain their children and have greater success in recruiting outsiders, the long-standing Christian monopoly is going to continue.

In the meantime, given the amount of religious assimilation that is taking place and may take place, the development that is well worth watching may not so much be the expanding of Canada's religious mosaic as the increasing cultural, social, and theological diversification of Catholicism and Protestantism.[18]

★★★

To sum up, for all the attention being given to the numbers being up for "Religious Nones," a variety of newer fringe groups, and other major world religions, it's important to again take note of Statistics Canada's lead headline for its census report: "Canada still predominantly Roman Catholic and Protestant."[19] The historically dominant Catholic and Protestant groups continue to enjoy a significant monopoly as "the market choice" of almost 8 in 10 (78%) of Canadians. In the long run, relatively few of their affiliates switch or drop out altogether.

TABLE 2.7. **Canada's Top 12 Religious Groups in 2001**

1. Roman Catholic	12,936,910	45%
2. United Church	2,839,125	12
3. Anglican	2,035,500	8
4. Christian *(unspecified)*	780,450	3
5. Baptist	729,475	3
6. Eastern Orthodox	606,620	2
7. Lutheran	606,590	2
8. Muslim	579,640	2
9. Protestant *(unspecified)*	549,205	2
10. Presbyterian	409,830	1
11. Pentecostal	369,480	1
12. Jewish	329,995	1

Source: Statistics Canada, 2001 Census.

What's more, it is not a monopoly those groups are about to lose. As we have seen, in addition to regaining many temporary "Nones" and benefiting greatly from religious assimilation patterns, Mainline Protestants and Roman Catholics – along with evangelical Protestants – have been showing signs of new life. An interesting point that Susan Catto made in the November 2003 *Time* magazine feature on religion was that Christian groups are demonstrating considerable creativity and flexibility as they attempt to respond to the diverse spiritual needs of Canadians. Churches are not sitting back and bowing to the competition. On the contrary, they are being aggressive in both creating milieus where people can be comfortable and meeting in familiar, non-threatening settings such as pubs, theatres and shopping malls. As Catto put it, "Religion in Canada is finding a home in unlikely places."[20]

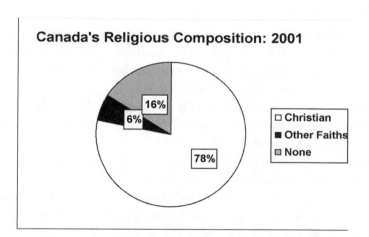

Canada's Religious Composition: 2001

16%
6%
78%

□ Christian
■ Other Faiths
▨ None

The Great Opportunity...and Responsibility

Think what these findings mean. Christians continue to dominate the Canadian religious scene. In addition, the two sources of potential attrition actually function as two tributaries that add to the size of the Christian river.

- Two in three people who say they have "no religion" will probably end up identifying with Christianity.
- Social and religious assimilation will see Christianity gain far more people from Other Faith groups than it loses.

In a society dominated by Catholics and Protestants, it is very difficult for people to stay "Nothing" across generations; their children have a maddening habit of socializing with and marrying "Somethings." ✓ Similarly, it is extremely difficult to be an "Other" when the social and marital choices are so limited, and the pull in the direction of cultural and religious conformity is so great. It all adds up to a remarkably advantageous position for Catholics and Protestants.

Canada's Demographic Reality

- *A Christian monopoly persists.*
- *It is fed by Nones and Other Religions.*
- *The mosaic is heavily Christian in nature.*

Claiming the Monopoly

Let's be honest: in a society such as ours, where we live by the creed of diversity and multiculturalism, Christians are extremely reluctant to claim a position of dominance and can be expected to be chastised if they do. Ironically, it has been far more fashionable, politically correct, and downright easier to be a shrinking tile in the mosaic. So it is that we are far more likely to hear Christian leaders, including theologians, telling us that this is no longer a Christian country, that Christian dominance is a thing of the past, that Christians are becoming less and less numerically prominent in an increasingly religiously diverse Canada.

Like it or not, the Christian numerical monopoly is a demographic reality that is not about to change in the foreseeable future. Such a reality has dramatically important implications for the role that Christian churches need to play in ensuring that the spiritual, personal, and social needs of Canadians are met.

A Post-Christian Canada?

- *Canada no longer Christian?*
- *Christianity no longer dominant?*
- *Christianity a Shrinking part of the mosaic?*

Claiming the Responsibility

Adding to the weight of that responsibility are the extensive research findings that document (a) the widespread *spiritual needs* of Canadians, (b) the fact that large numbers of people *find life difficult* and could often use some help, and (c) the supreme importance that we all place on *good relationships*, yet that we frequently find elusive.

Currently, in the course of addressing such needs, about 25% of Canadians are fairly actively involved in churches. But what is stunning is that *almost half of the remaining 75%* of the population – adults and teenagers alike – say they are open to greater involvement.

TABLE 2.8. **Receptivity to Greater Involvement**

*"Would you consider the possibility of being more involved in a religious group if you found it to be worthwhile for yourself or your family?"**

PEOPLE ATTENDING LESS THAN MONTHLY

	Adults	Teens
NATIONALLY	55%	39
Roman Catholics	56	46
Quebec	55	41
Outside Quebec	56	51
Protestants	64	47
Mainline	63	44
Conservative	73	55
Other Faiths	67	48
None	34	21

**"For yourself or your family" was omitted in the youth survey.*
Source: Bibby, Restless Gods, 2004:50.

- The levels are fairly consistent across all religious families, including Quebec Catholics.
- In addition, indicative of latent identification among Religious Nones, some 30% of adults and 20% of teens who say they have no religion nonetheless acknowledge that they are willing to consider becoming involved in religious groups.

What an opportunity! What a responsibility.

The Big "If"

But there's a major catch. We all know that – quiz shows and lotteries aside – nothing comes easy in life. The current religious situation is no exception. I, like you, have been around long enough to know that many church leaders are looking for simple and easy solutions when it comes to seeing churches and parishes grow. One Baptist official told me four years ago that he found many of the congregations he dealt with were looking for "magic potions": the program that works, the music that brings people in, and so on. I'm convinced he's right. In Canada the potions often take the form of hints and formulas imported from the U.S., sometimes from England, occasionally from places like Germany. The naive assumption is that if they work "there," they will work here. For too long, too many churches have wasted time and resources on magic potions. We've got to do better.

Replacing Magic with Ministry

We followed up that question about receptivity with the obvious tough question: *"What kind of things would make it worthwhile?"* Responses were open-ended. People across the country were very clear about the number one motivating factor: *ministry.* They spoke first and foremost about being receptive to greater involvement if religious groups could help them deal with their spiritual needs, cope with personal issues, and have better ties with their partners and their children. The number-two and number-three factors pertained to their desire for organizational changes and some personal versus church–related factors respectively.

What Kinds of Things People Say Would Make it Worthwhile for Them to Be More Involved in a Religious Group

Ministry Factors (40%)

"...support and comfort...a strong moral environment...firmer direction...provide peace of mind...help me find a job for my spouse...address social, emotional, and health concerns...support during tragic times...if it added to the well-being of my children and family...greater friendship and togetherness...if I felt that I could grow as a spiritual person...be more attuned to everyday community well-being...if it would make people happy...if it were fun and fulfilling...relating to my life more closely...more down-to-earth approach to everyday problems...if religion dealt more with the reality of problems we experience and how to cope...having help looking after elderly parents...spiritual deepening..."

Organizational Factors (30%)

"...enjoyable services...more open to modern culture and issues facing people today...less abstract...treat all people as equal...allow priests to marry...interactive programs...dropping the formality and ceremony, and bringing it down to the human level...recognize that women are significant...less involvement in controversial social issues...make it interesting, try new things...a strong focus on spirituality, greater acceptance of and harmony with other religious groups, less politics and power struggles..."

Respondent Factors (30%)

"...being married and raising a family...having more time...if my kids lived with me...my family becoming more involved with church activities...if I had children I might consider Sunday School so they would learn and understand something of their heritage...will likely be more involved as my kids become involved...a change in my shift work...couldn't tell you – just seems that at some point it will be the right thing for my family..."

Source: Derived from Bibby, Restless Gods, *2004:224.*

In addressing the question of why participation levels are so low when levels of identification are so high, many observers point in rote-like fashion to cultural explanations, such as secularization, modernization, and postmodernism. Others often emphasize indifference and disenchantment. However, I would argue that most such interpretations are applicable to only small segments of the Canadian population. They don't explain why the people who are involved are involved, and why so many additional people are open to greater involvement.

It seems to me that, when we look at the Canadian population as a whole, the research findings are decisive. The *demand* for ministries that emphasize spiritual, personal, and relational issues is there. The problem is that, in too many instances, the *supplier* has not come through. Simply put, Canadians readily indicate that they have spiritual interests and needs, are experiencing various problems as they live out everyday life, and value good relationships more than anything else. Churches that could touch their lives spiritually, personally, and relationally are churches to which they would be drawn.

In one word, Canadians are open to churches that have *significance*. My research into why people are involved in groups such as the Anglican and United churches and the Christian and Missionary Alliance has led to a relatively simple conclusion: they are people who say that the Christian faith and local congregational involvement enrich their lives.[21] Faith and church have significance. That's why involvement is worth their time and resources.

But what should also be evident from all the research we have been examining is that Canadians are not open to just any churches that minister well. The findings clearly show that the vast majority of people who are receptive to greater involvement are looking in the direction of the groups of their parents and grandparents. These are the groups with which they identify. To the extent that a significant renaissance of organized religion in Canada will take place, it can be expected to heavily follow identification lines – whereby Catholics reach Catholics, Mainline Protestants reach Mainline Protestants, and Conservative Protestants reach Conservative Protestants. The reality of ongoing religious identification appears to be a great gift from God. But it calls for very good stewardship of those identification lines, including an unprecedented level of cooperative ministry that ensures those lines of affinity are used well. I will return to these issues shortly.

Restless Gods and Restless Churches

There is little doubt about it. The evidence suggests that God has been at work in Canadian life, preparing people, awakening them, relating to them. There also is reason to believe that God has been at work in Canadian churches, awakening them to the interests, needs, and receptivity of the millions of people with whom they have limited contact.

At this point in history, those who value Christian faith are look-ing out at large numbers of affiliates through a remarkable window of opportunity. What's needed is an effective response. The problem most groups have had is not that people have been dropping out or switching. In many instances, groups have lost the luxury of their immigration pipelines or, in the case of Quebec, the luxury of a captive audience. As a result, they have needed to sustain numbers by doing what they should be doing: ministering to their people. The data suggest that to the extent they have experienced numerical problems, it's not because the needs and interests of their affiliates have disappeared. Rather, groups have been coming up short on ministry – especially effective ministry to chil-dren, young adults, and young families.

That has to change. And it can. If it doesn't, many churches will continue to go broke and many people will continue to go hungry. At that point, God may well decide to scrap the current renovation pro-gram and try some new organizational alternatives.

But until further notice, it appears that "the plan" is for the nation's dominant churches to play a major role in the renaissance of religion in Canada. As Don Posterski and Andrew Grenville recently put it, "Clearly, many Canadians believe in God, God believes in the Church. To bring these two realities together is the challenge, and the opportunity, for the Canadian Church in the new century."[22]

Recognizing Four Major Implications for Ministry

To the sociologist who tries to call things the way they are, yet is also open to the possibility of the activity of God, the current Canadian religious situation points to at least four major implications for ministry.

1. The Need to Rediscover God

It seems strange to have to say it, but it needs to be said: it's not only social scientists who are inclined to interpret much of what is happening in the world without an explicit sense of the activity of God. Religious leaders frequently join social analysts in interpreting what is going on in individual lives by lining up a predictable range of social, cultural, and psychological explanations to explain things such as belief levels, the nature of religious experience, and declining levels of participation in organized religion. As United Church minister Rob Oliphant recently put it, "The church has gone so far to the reason side that we are out of balance; we are losing our capacity to appreciate God's glory, God's awe, and we have eliminated the sense of mystery."[1]

God in the Lives of Individuals

I have been arguing that when 80% of Canadians believe in a God who cares about them personally – some three to four times the number of weekly service attenders – it's worth considering the possibility that such belief may not have its origin solely in individuals, groups, and culture. When almost 50% consistently claim that they have experienced God's presence during a period in our history when regular attendance is only half that high, maybe – just maybe – there is something going on that has been eluding the empirical eye. And when some three in four of those adults whom we routinely see in stores and pass on streets acknowledge that they pray privately – one in two of them weekly or more – such an unheralded and, frankly, surprising reality should at least make us wonder if a Source has been at work that readily transcends mere religious socialization.

In short, as I said earlier, the prevalence of belief, experience, prayer, and spiritual quest in the lives of so many Canadians of all ages may mean that God has been stirring in the lives of people across the country. Perhaps God has grown impatient with the churches, and has chosen to accelerate a supplementary but more effective strategy: relating to people directly.

Regardless of whether you agree with the specifics of what I am saying, if you are someone who values Christian faith, you know that a central tenet of the tradition has been the belief that God is at work in the world, including in individual lives. That basic idea, I am suggesting, is frequently minimized in favour of personal and cultural explanations of what is taking place.

God in the Lives of Churches

Such an a-theistic posture, it seems to me, was particularly evident when we were trying to understand what was happening to the Church in the post-1950s. Commentator after commentator spoke of the demise of organized religion in the course of consciously and unconsciously buying into the secularization argument. The prevalent responses of Canada's Christian groups appear to have been along the following lines.

- *Roman Catholics* seem to have accepted the reality of secularization, particularly in view of having experienced it so acutely in Quebec, but nonetheless maintained that the Church would prevail.
- *Mainline Protestants* also accepted the fact that secularization was occurring, but, particularly in the case of the United Church, felt the appropriate response was for churches to function as faithful remnants.[2]

- *Conservative Protestants* were also inclined to recognize the pervasiveness of secularization, but tended to decry it and maintain that it needed to be reversed.

Looking back, I have one simple question: "Where was God in all of this?" As Mainliners and Quebec Catholics experienced involvement declines, as the participation losses of the Catholic Church in the rest of Canada were being masked by the lifeline of immigration, as evangelical churches started to buck the attrition patterns – where was God? Were the developments that were taking place simply due to cultural and organizational factors? Had God, for example, given up on the established Canadian churches? God seemed absent.

I would venture to say that, as recently as the early 1990s, relatively few people in Canada were expecting the well-entrenched religious groups to experience a reversal of numerical fortunes. Almost no one would have predicted that a denomination such as the United Church would, in the early years of the 21st century, be giving premiere attention to themes such as spirituality, Bible study, youth ministry, healing, and personal transformation – themes that are currently commonplace nationally, congregationally, and in theological and lay education settings.[3] There was talk in the 1990s about the Anglican Church, at the national level, having to declare bankruptcy. One diocese was forced to take that route. Things looked bleak. Yet in the early years of the new century, at parish levels, the Anglican Church – though hardly without its controversies, notably the same-sex marriage issue – is exhibiting much life. Lutherans and Presbyterians are also exhibiting down-and-up local vitality patterns.

From the standpoint of the organizational analyst looking on, such developments could be viewed as fairly predictable phases in the life cycles of long-standing organizations. But for the believer, what is happening in the churches is not something that is taking place "all by itself." If God had a reason for bringing Canadian churches into being in the first place, it seems reasonable to assume that some major new developments – especially those that were not anticipated – may well reflect the ongoing activity and purposes of God.

And so I have been suggesting to you that what we may be witnessing as we see people continuing to identify with the country's dominant groups and see intriguing signs of new life in those groups is something more than mere personal and organizational developments. We may be witnessing the activity of a God who is opting to continue to make significant use of Canada's long-established religious bodies to reach out to Canadians.

My more important point – beyond my precarious personal reflections on possible Divine activity – is that Christian leaders need to be acutely sensitive to the fact that what is occurring in the churches is not only "of us." United Church authors Christopher White and Donna Sinclair are among those who call for such sensitivity. In reflecting on new life in Mainline Protestantism and beyond, they raise the question "How was it possible that a God of life would want God's church to wither away?" Recalling the Emmaus Road experience, they further ask, "What if we are like [them and] simply do not realize that the Spirit of God remains with us, in our congregations? What if we are in the early stages of a religious and social reawakening?" White and Sinclair add, "The tough decades are far from over. But we confidently declare that the church will be reborn, and that the new birth will start with local congregations."[4]

In times of apparent decline or possible revitalization, God needs to be viewed as "in the midst." Developments in Canada that have caught most of us by surprise point to the possibility that God is centrally involved in what is taking place.

As readers know well, such recognition of God's presence and sensitivity to God's purposes historically has given meaning to ministry and empowered Christians and their congregations. It is no less important in our day. Allowing for "the God factor" adds a whole new dimension and a whole new dynamic to what is going on.

It also makes for a far more interesting reading of developments: past, present, and future. Take Quebec, for example. Recently, the Vice-Dean of the Faculty of Theology at Laval University, Professor Gilles Routhier, told *Time* magazine, "I think the Catholic Church is still in purgatory in Quebec. After we turned on Catholicism, we didn't invest in other spiritual or religious roads." Routhier suggested that people are being attracted to materialism, secularism, and even Quebec nationalism. Dr. Glenn Smith, the director of a Montreal-based Protestant urban ministry, added, "There's a massive rejection of institutional faith. I don't think people will return."[5]

A Minister Who Rediscovered God

In 1963, at the age of 25, I was ordained in the Presbyterian Church in Canada and was appointed for a one-year term to what was then known as Goforth Memorial Presbyterian Church in Saskatoon, a new congregation with a new building.

Soon I discovered that the optimism of the 1950s and early 1960s about the life and future of the church gave way to pessimism. As I looked at the membership statistics for the Mainline denominations, it seemed to me that large portions of that membership, as if on cue, decided that in 1964 they would no longer attend church! Both from outside and from within the church there were increasingly loud voices that told us that God was dead, that the church was no longer relevant and would wither away unless somehow it adapted to the "new world" we were entering.

One Sunday, some time in 1966 or thereabouts, deeply depressed after another week of being assaulted with bad news, I preached a "bad news sermon," reflecting somehow this dark mood of pessimism that hung around us all. After the service, the 70 or so members and adherents filed past me as I shook their hands. They looked downcast. It was not a good Sunday.

Now, there was a couple in that congregation who had come from the United States. Mrs. Horowitz became a member of the choir and taught Sunday School. Her husband, Aaron, was Head of the Veterinary Science Department at the university. Although Aaron was not a member, he faithfully attended services with his wife and joined the choir. They must have been in their mid-40s when I knew them. He was a non-practicing Jew.

That Sunday, after my dark tirade and after almost everyone had left, I noticed Aaron waiting to have a word with me. I noticed deep emotion on his face. He shook my hand and then, with tears rolling down his cheeks, he said, "Tony, why did you do this? You have a most wonderful message to proclaim that people need to hear. You have a message from a living God. Tell that story, Tony. Please, don't ever talk like that again." He gave me a big hug and left me standing dumbfounded and humbled. This "son of the covenant," not formally part of the Christian community, gave voice to God's Word to me.

This encounter changed my life as a minister. As I look back over 40 years of ministry, I shall be forever grateful to God for Aaron Horowitz, who reminded me that ministry is not about me, myself, and I – not even about the institutional church – but is all about God. And God will do what God will do.

And, by the way, soon I will be receiving that pension people thought we preachers would never receive!

Rev. Tony Plomp, former moderator of the Presbyterian Church in Canada.

But suppose God decided to shake up the Roman Catholic Church in Quebec – and to shake up Quebeckers? Would the situation continue to be as carved in stone as Routhier and Smith suggest? You know the answer. There is a great need to rediscover the activity of God, a rediscovery that introduces limitless possibilities.

2. The Need to Understand and Utilize Religious Identification

If I were asked what is my *one* single most important finding after 30 years of studying religion in Canada, I wouldn't hesitate with my response: it's the reality of ongoing religious identification.

An Underused Concept

Like many of you – especially those of you who are Protestant – I grew up assuming that if people said they were "United" or "Anglican" or "Catholic" yet seldom went to church, what they said meant nothing. It was just a way of sidestepping an inquiry, such as from a Jehovah's Witness, that allowed people to close their front doors rather than slam them.

Many church leaders continue to assume that identification without involvement essentially means nothing. For example, when learning that the 2001 census had uncovered some 70,000 Anglicans in the Ottawa-Hull area versus the 35,000 who show up for services, Anglican bishop Peter Coffin told Bob Harvey of the *Ottawa Citizen* that the census findings have nothing to do with reality.[6] Similarly, Elizabeth Bowen, president of the Canadian Unitarian Council, told *Time* that "we were a bit surprised" to learn that the census located 18,000 people who identified themselves as Unitarian, since "we have about 5,200 members that we know of."[7] In the case of Protestants and Catholics, some observers attempt to resolve this disparity between "what people say and what they do" by referring to them as "cultural Christians."[8]

Such a dismissal of religious self-identification is extremely poor science and horrible pastoral practice. If people say they are "Anglican" or "Unitarian" or "Catholic" or "Nazarene," then that's how they see themselves. In a social and psychological and emotional sense, that's what they are. People don't arbitrarily claim identification with religious traditions. They're not one day "Catholic" and the next day "United" and another day "Pentecostal." We're not talking about hockey and Leaf or Canadien or Oiler bandwagons here.

- We're talking about religious self-designations that provide us with extremely important clues about people's personal and family religious histories, as well as their religious memories.
- How people view themselves religiously has highly significant implications for their religious comfort zones – the groups with which they feel a measure of affinity versus the ones that they regard as foreign and maybe even a bit strange.

Identification as a Key Ministry Asset

It's one thing for religious leaders to get an "F" for their scientific inaccuracy in downplaying "religious I.D." It's quite another thing for them to develop policies and programs that are oblivious to it. That's downright irresponsible. It's like organizations that want to relate to immigrants ignoring their national and cultural backgrounds.

A religious group with which people identify clearly has a significant *competitive advantage* over other groups – the advantage of being able to have *access* to sizable numbers of what we have been referring to as its "affiliates." Identification represents potential affinity, potential familiarity.

- If a person thinks she's a Roman Catholic, then Catholics are in a better position than any other group in the country to have an initial conversation with her.
- The same is true of a person who thinks he's Lutheran: the Lutherans are more likely to get a hearing than any other religious group in Canada.
- And so it goes for the advantages that Baptists have in dealing with people who say they are Baptists, Presbyterians with self-proclaimed Presbyterians, Anglicans with Anglicans. You get the picture.

Conversely, to the extent that groups ignore the significance of religious self-identification, they fail to recognize their *competitive disadvantage*. Because they make the error of equating lack of involvement with disaffiliation, they make the further error of assuming that the uninvolved are ripe for recruitment. What the research shows is that most people are already "taken." When they are asked, they say that (a) they identify with a group and (b) they are not interested in switching. That's putting things pretty plain.]

Does all this sound fairly obvious? Of course it is. Yet it's a reality that seems to inform relatively few religious groups and individual churches across the land. I would go so far as to say that, to the extent Canada's churches attempt to reach people outside their walls, they give more time and money to pursuing mysterious and nebulous individuals whom they variously label "the lost," "seekers," "the community," and "the world" than they do their own people. In reality, the vast majority of Canadians who are "lost" or "seeking" or comprise "the community" and certainly the accessible "world" are...guess who? Catholics, United Churchers, Anglicans, Lutherans, Presbyterians, and evangelicals who have slipped out of the sight of their churches. Groups that are committed to effective outreach surely will have the good sense to at least start by finding their own people.

By all means they can be and should be more enterprising. But pursuing their own folk is a pretty good and logical place to start. That's where "the competitive advantage" clearly lies. Anyone who has any doubts needs to have a short conversation with outreach-minded groups such as Jehovah's Witnesses and Mormons, who would love to be able to work from such an enviable point of affinity.

It's time we stopped treating the religious identification reality as if it were a mystery. Does anyone need to be reminded that the best bet for ethnic church growth is to follow ethnic lines plus religious identification lines – that a Chinese Alliance church would be expected to draw large numbers of recruits from the evangelical Asian community, or that Korean congregations owe much of their viability to being able to recruit immigrants from Korea?[9] Unless I'm missing something, ethnic church leaders take such affinity lines as a given, and use them as a major means of recruitment. If that's the case, then why should we act bewildered by the simple assertion that religious families need to similarly utilize identification lines of affinity?

I again remind readers that it's not just that the churches lose out by failing to take the concept of identification seriously. That's bad enough. What's worse is that when groups dismiss the salience of religious identification, they essentially desert their affiliates. Because their people are (a) not being pursued by their own groups and (b) typically wary of alternative groups, most of them fall between the cracks when it comes to ministry.

The Price Some Abandoned Affiliates Pay

It's a true story. A couple in Edmonton – whom I will call "Lorraine and Larry" – grew up Baptist. Both were baptized, were married in the church, and attended frequently up until around the time they had their first child. At that point they seemed to lose interest, attended sporadically, and then stopped attending altogether.

Surprisingly, their fairly large church made little contact with them – in part, it seems, because their drop-off coincided with a pastoral change. During the first 10 years or so of their marriage, Lorraine and Larry encountered tragedy in the form of losing two sets of twins who were stillborn. Over the years, Lorraine had a number of minor health problems. Later, their ties with their daughter-in-law and grandson were jolted when their son opted out of the marriage. As they moved into their '60s, they – like so many others – struggled to deal with their aging and dying parents. Larry found out he had cancer.

Now, through all this, their Baptist church was taking pride in its growth and outreach efforts, making use of popular programs that spanned Evangelism Explosion in the 1970s through the Alpha Program in recent years. All along, Lorraine and Larry lived in the same home, some four blocks from the church. They continued to see themselves as Baptists. Their names remained on the church membership list for years; at worst they presumably had eventually been relegated to the archives.

Yet, unbelievably, as the years and decades went by, Lorraine and Larry weren't contacted by the church…not to merely get them to "come back to church," but just to see if they were okay. On a number of occasions, such a simple act of caring would have been so timely, so poignant, so moving – not to mention so badly needed. But it was never made.

What adds to the tragedy of this story is that it is hardly unique to this Baptist church. It could just as readily be a story, which, with minor alterations in names and specifics, is told by affiliates of so many Catholic and Protestant churches across the country. Things have to change.

Learning to "Think Affiliate and Concentric"[10]

For too long, Canadian religious groups have been stuck in a paradigm rut where they have viewed people in dichotomous, black-and-white terms. Reflecting both ecclesiology and theology, they have variously tended to divide individuals into two categories: *active* and *inactive, saved* and *unsaved, involved* and *uninvolved, good* and *lapsed, lost* and *found, saint* and *sinner.* American thinkers have added to the confusion by disseminating the idea that people are either *churched* or *unchurched.* A popular children's chorus dating back many years to my Sunday School days (see the power of religious memory?) comes to mind:

> *One door and only one, and yet the sides are two.*
> *I'm on the inside, on which side are you?*

Our findings on the ongoing importance of religious identification suggest that it would be far more helpful to think of people who identify with groups as "affiliates" who have varying degrees of involvement. Rather than viewing them as "churched" or "unchurched," for example, it is more accurate to see them, as actives affiliates, marginal affiliates, inactive affiliates, and disaffiliates. While these categories obviously are fairly arbitrary, *actives* might be viewed as people who attend every week, *marginals* as those who are bi-monthly to monthly attenders, and *inactive* affiliates as individuals who attend less than monthly. *Disaffiliates* would refer to people who describe themselves as having no religion, but come from homes where their parents were either Catholic or Protestant.

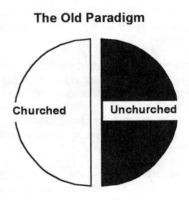

The Old Paradigm

Churched   Unchurched

The New Paradigm: A Concentric Model of Affiliates

Actives

Marginals

Inactives

Disaffiliates

What is important here is to see people who identify with a religious group as part of that group's pool of people, regardless of their level of participation. Because of their self-proclaimed ties, it's essential that they be included in the pool. Obviously such a model differs radically from assuming that if people are not highly involved, they are religious free agents – lost to their identification groups and prime candidates for recruitment by the religious competition.

In sharp contrast to that kind of thinking, a concentric model depicts affiliates who identify as part of the overall religious group. Moreover, those in the pool who are less involved constitute the primary target of the group's ministry to Canadians who are seemingly "outside" the church. The people on the outer ring – the "disaffiliates" – remain in the pool for a very good reason. As we saw when we looked at "Religious Nones," many of these people are younger adults who are temporarily "disaffiliated." Far from being lost to groups, a large number will "reaffiliate" in the course of turning to the religious groups of their parents for rites of passage.

In case anyone is confused, let me emphasize one last time that the need to more clearly understand religious self-identification is not driven by academic quibbling. It is of paramount significance. It is the key bridge to Canadians who are not highly involved in congregations.

Simply the Best Place to Start

Does this mean that Canada's religious groups begin and end only with people who identify with them? Of course not. I have frequently told the story of having a Mennonite leader in Indiana rise to his feet during a question–and–answer session and remind me, "Professor Bibby," [I know I am in trouble when someone calls me "Professor" – like when teachers in days of yore called me "Reginald"] "Mennonites do not fulfill the Great Commission by only going after Mennonites." My response back then is the same today: "I'm not trying to tell you where to stop – I'm just trying to tell you where to start."

If churches are ever going to connect with Canadians who need ministry in a comprehensive way, it's imperative that they follow lines of affinity. That's the only way that most will ever get a hearing. Of course, groups are free to reach out to non–affiliates. No one is saying they should not minister generously to those who are needing and willing to receive their ministry.

By all means, when they have exhausted their affiliate pools, they should move on to other people with whom they have affinity. When Anglicans, for example, have exhausted their leads with active Anglicans, they can move on to less–active Lutherans, Roman Catholics, United Church individuals, and Presbyterians. When those leads are also exhausted, they can go after infrequently attending Conservative Protestants, people in Other Faith groups, and the lifelong Nones. But groups have to start somewhere. And the best place to start is with people who think they are part of one's religious group.

No one is naive enough to think every affiliate will be receptive to ministry. The Project Canada findings, for example, suggest that, at the outset, about one person in two will be receptive, and therefore one in two will not. We all know that religious identification means very different things to different people. While many place positive importance on identification groups, a good number of others identify without exactly being sure why. There also are some whose affiliation line has deteriorated to a tattered thread, where they identify but want little to do with a group because of such things as bad experiences, abuse and scandal, or feel they have "graduated" from "that kind of religion."[11] There are also many people who are not totally clear on "what they are" because their parents, other family members, or they themselves have had a measure of involvement with more than one group.

Some Examples of Varied Identification Lines

- Tenacious…loyalty is intense.
- Tenuous…importance not all that conscious.
- Tattered…fragile; anger, anguish, alienation present.
- Tangled…different IDs for parents, partners, self.

Source: Derived from Bibby, There's Got to Be More! *1995:42-43*

Still, following identification lines is too obvious an opportunity for connection to be ignored. Canada's religious groups consequently need to take explicit and systematic steps to locate those people who are identifying with them. If such religious identification "leads" do not turn out to be helpful in finding and responding to a given individual, so be it. In such instances, one group doesn't have any "market advantage." That would take things back to essentially where we are now, where everyone theoretically goes after "the unchurched."

And where's God in all this? Probably in the midst. Identification lines may be one of God's largely untapped gifts to the country's religious groups, offered as critically important leads for making contact with Canadians. The identification lines are something like unused telephone lines. It's time to connect them and see what can happen.

The Mandate to Find Affiliates

There are few biblical precedents for chopping people from church lists or other-wise giving up on them – let alone ostracizing them for not showing up enough or not contributing to the church financially. There are, however, stories of shep-herds going out after lost sheep, houses being swept for lost coins, and, of course, this classic about a father and an affiliate of sorts who disappeared for a while, but came back. A cause for pause is that no one had gone searching for him, and not everyone was happy to see him.

Then Jesus said, *"There was a man who had two sons. The younger son gath-ered all that he had and travelled to a distant country, and there he squandered his property. When he had spent everything, he began to be in need. But when he came to himself, he set off and went to his father. While he was still far off, his father saw him and was filled with compassion; he ran and put his arms around him and kissed him. 'This son of mine was dead and is alive again.' And they began to celebrate.*

"Now his elder son became angry. Then the father said to him, 'Son you are always with me, and all that is mine is yours. But we had to celebrate and rejoice, because this brother of yours was dead and has come to life; he was lost and has been found.'"

Source: *Taken from Luke 15:11–32 (NRSV)*

3. It's All About Ministry

When people talk about the problems of organized religion in Canada, invariably they focus on numbers. Alarm and chagrin are ex-pressed about attendance and membership being down. Both insiders and outsiders murmur about what can be done to "get people to come to church" and to "bring people back." Put in perspective, it often sounds as if people have run away from some unpleasant home, and what we now have to figure out is how to lure them back – in part because we need help in paying the bills.

Who Cares if the Pews are Emptier?

In the light of what we know from the research, let me state my take on all this explicitly: if the numbers are down, the problem is not empty pews *per se*. The problem lies with inadequate ministry. The solu-tion does not lie merely in finding ways to put bottoms back in the pews, including gimmicks, door prizes, and the like – and certainly not with magic potions. It lies with effective ministry.

It's not all that complex. We give our lives and our resources to the things we define as significant. No one has to plead with us to spend time on work that we enjoy or with people who enrich our lives. We need only the soft sell of a flyer to head off to the mall to buy that new printer or that new piece of furniture. We don't need to be coaxed to watch the hockey final (especially if we are men) or figure-skating championships (especially if we are women). We don't have to be threatened into giving a few bucks or even a few hours to that charity we think is important.

Let's be clear once and for all: people who are involved in churches are people who have found significance in churches. They and the faith and the God that are central to the churches add something – often a great deal – to their lives. To the extent Canadians find that churches touch their lives in significant ways, they will want to be associated with them. Conversely, to the extent they do not, they can be expected to stay away. I have documented such a conclusion in major studies of the United Church, Anglicans, Presbyterians, and evangelicals, including the Christian and Missionary Alliance.[12] In the case of Roman Catholics, respected American researchers William D'Antonio, James Davidson, Dean Hoge, and Katherine Meyer recently summed up the situation this way:

> All analysts agree that the centrality of any element is a product of how it has served the genuine needs of the person in the past. Over time, the Church and the faith become central to people who experience deep gratification and affirmation from them – spiritual, intellectual, and social. It follows that Catholic teaching, especially to the young, must have these goals and must avoid negative appeals to obligation, duty, or guilt.[13]

Frankly, I don't know that God cares all that much about churches and their numerical problems as such. I have no doubt, however, that God is more than slightly troubled if those empty pews mean that churches are failing to minister to people – if empty pews point to a significant number of people who have emptier lives.

The research is indicting.

- More than 20 million people currently identify with Catholicism and Protestantism.
- Some seven million of them are actively involved in churches.
- However, approximately 12 million are attending services less than once a month.
- More than six million of these infrequent attenders say they are open to greater involvement, *if* they found it to be worthwhile for themselves or their families.
- What would make it worthwhile? As we saw, most people say ministry that is responsive to their spiritual, personal, and relational needs. Many also would like churches be open to making some structural adjustments that, for the most part, sound pretty reasonable to me.

TABLE 3.1. **Receptivity to Greater Involvement by Region, Gender, and Age**

"Would you consider the possibility of being more involved in a religious group if you found it to be worthwhile for yourself or your family?" ★

PEOPLE ATTENDING LESS THAN MONTHLY	
NATIONALLY	55%
British Columbia	45
Prairies	62
Ontario	58
Quebec	50
Atlantic	64
Women	55
Men	55
18–34	59
35–54	55
55 and over	48

Source: Bibby, Project Canada 2000.

The message such findings offer concerning the performance of churches is not exactly subtle. As a result, all those empty pews must be pretty upsetting to you know Who.

Mistaking the Road for the Destination

In the course of carrying out research for *Unknown Gods* a decade or so ago, I came across two stories that are worth repeating in the current context. One is part of marketing lore; the second is becoming part of church lore.

A company that made drill bits went out of business. The company couldn't understand what happened. It felt confident that it had been making the best drill bits in the world. However, what the company was too slow to realize was that their customers didn't want drill bits; they wanted a hole in the ground. Consequently, when another product came along that made a better hole for less money, their customers went elsewhere.[14]

Canadians are longing for God and ministry, not churches. If the primary goal of churches is simply to get people to come through their front doors, they will be like companies making outdated drill bits. The pews will continue to be anything but full. And God may have to consider some company options.

The church story is about the New Westminster Anglican Diocese in Vancouver – how it embarked on a program around 1990 to make contact with "lapsed" Anglicans and other people with spiritual interests but no formal church ties. A well-planned campaign was carried out, complete with creative ads that appeared in community newspapers and posters that were placed in stores and other public places. One poster, for example, showed a young boy in an uncomfortable shirt and tie with the caption, "Does religion give you a pain in the neck?" It went on to say that people might be surprised how much the Church has changed, inviting people to "come prepared to relax, free from life's restrictions, and let the most important part of you breathe again." The posters carried the slogan "Show your spirit. Come back to church." They came complete with a 1-800 number. The communications officer back then, Lorie Chortyk, told me that about the time everything was ready to roll, a secretary in the office posed a poignant and sobering question: "But what do we do if someone calls?"[15]

So what if the church is full? Good promotion, a major concert, a renowned speaker or a world-class organist – not to mention extraordinary door prizes – could probably accomplish that. An exotic building could also probably do the trick. But Douglas John Hall, reflecting on the period in United Church history when the building of churches seemed to be the denomination's reason for being, astutely writes, "The pomposity of our entrepreneurial building stage has been chastened by the knowledge that pretty churches cannot sustain congregations."[16] The same could be said for the "gate attractions" I mentioned. What will bring people out and keep them coming is the realization that they are in a place that is able to deliver on the promise of good ministry. That has to be the focus of churches that aspire to touch the lives of their affiliates.

The Numbers Will Take Care of Themselves

There is no need to get into silly debates about the importance or lack of importance of numbers. Numbers and integrity are not polar opposites. From an organizational point of view, congregations need a certain number of active members in order to be viable. That said, if churches minister well to people, they can be expected to grow – at least to the extent of embracing the people around them.

Jesus' ministry again serves as an example.[17] As he moved among the people of his time, he obviously received diverse responses. Yet, as he ministered to the various needs of those he encountered, "multitudes," we are told, followed him. Of course he experienced opposition, indifference, and hostility. Still, because his message and ministry hit a responsive chord, people followed him. His ministry was not about growth, but growth was an outcome of his ministry.

Rev. Cheri DiNovo, under whose leadership the inner-city Emmanuel–Howard Park United Church in Toronto has experienced significant new life and growth since the late 1990s, has summed up the ministry-growth reality this way: "How do you be the church to people who are hungry? It's simple: you feed them."[18] Catholic leaders and experts attending a March 2004 Vatican meeting to discuss ways the Church could address growing indifference to religion and faith communities came to a similar conclusion. In the words of one cardinal from Indonesia, "We must deal with real values and the deep concerns about life." The running of schools and hospitals is important, but the cardinal added, "Without living the real experience of Christian love, there will be no conversion." He added, "The new evangelization must be driven by love. If we have no love, we will draw no people."[19]

To the extent that people find significance in churches – find that their lives are touched by responses to their fundamental spiritual, personal, and social needs – there is every reason to believe that many will want to be part of those churches. If ministry is there, the numbers will follow.

A Sell-Out to Consumers?

In almost every setting where I attempt to present such ideas, invariably someone raises a hand or nabs me during a break and asks the important question along these lines: "Aren't churches that respond to the interests and needs of Canadians coming precariously close to simply responding to consumer demand? People want and need this and that, and churches come through. Surely the call to Christian faith involves more than having one's needs met. It also involves a decision to commit one's life to Christ, give of one's time and money, grow in the faith, and engage in service to others."

They are right. However, if we again look at the ministry of Jesus, we see a ministry that typically involved an initial response to highly diversified needs: healing the sick, feeding the hungry, showing men where to fish, raising the dead, teaching people how to maximize life, making sure there was enough wine at a wedding, telling one person that he needed to experience a rebirth. Ministry was an entry point. Because Jesus' ministry touched people, many followed him, grew as disciples, and, in turn, shared in ministry to others. That, it seems to me, is the model churches should follow.

Over time, people who are ministered to are taught about the nature and expectations of Christian faith, and are encouraged to become committed followers and to grow in the faith. A major expectation from the outset is that people who have been ministered to will in turn share in efforts to minister to others.

One final note on ministry. In our Project Canada 2000 national survey, we asked people, "Do you think that religious groups still have a role to play in Canadian lives?" Some 76% of affiliates across the country indicated "Yes"; 51% of non-affiliates ("Nones") also said groups have a role to play. Asked what they consider that role to be, close to one half of Canada's affiliates responded that religious groups should address all of life. Relatively small proportions feel the role of groups should be limited only to *spiritual* matters, or to just *spiritual and personal* or *spiritual and social* issues.

TABLE 3.2. **Affiliates' Views of the Role Groups Should Be Playing by Attendance and Religious Family***

	All of Life	Spiritual Only	Spiritual & Personal	Spiritual & Social	No Role	Totals
NATIONALLY	46%	16	9	8	21	100
Weekly	70	14	7	5	4	100
Monthly	61	13	6	11	9	100
Yearly	37	17	10	9	27	100
Never	27	25	5	8	35	100
Conservative Protestants	68	11	7	4	10	100
Mainline Protestants	49	16	11	8	16	100
RCs: Outside Quebec	49	19	9	6	17	100
RCs: Quebec	36	13	6	10	35	100
Other Faiths	29	31	12	7	21	100
None	23	17	7	4	49	100

Source: Bibby, Project Canada 2000, and Restless Gods, 2004:188.

*Respondents were asked, "Do you think that religious groups still have a role to play in Canadian lives?" If they said "Yes," they then were asked if that role should be to address (1) all of life – spiritual, personal, and social issues, (2) spiritual and personal issues – staying out of social issues, (3) spiritual and social issues – staying out of personal issues, or (4) spiritual issues only.

These findings suggest that the wide diversity of interests and needs leaves the door pretty wide open for religious groups to do what they know they have to do in the course of attempting to minister with integrity: bring faith to bear on all of life.

However, the major asterisk mustn't be forgotten: the vast majority of people who indicate receptivity are not looking to just any group for ministry that touches their lives. They are not open to just any provider and certainly not even the best provider.

They are looking for ministry from the groups with which they identify.

4. It Can't Be Done Alone

One of the most blatant implications of the research is that a concerted, successful effort to reach out to Canadians who are not actively involved in the churches cannot possibly be done by only one group. The problem is not only a resource problem. It's an access problem.

Individual Groups Have Limited Reach

The access issue can be clarified by recalling the findings on switching. As we have seen, Canadians who identify with specific religious groups are not inclined to switch, despite both the assumption among Protestants that people can be recruited and the failure of those same groups to successfully recruit large numbers of people from other religious families.

TABLE 3.3. **Canada's "Religious Families"** *Approximate % of the Canadian Population★*	
Roman Catholics Outside Quebec	23%
Roman Catholics in Quebec	20
Mainline Protestants	23
United (12), Anglican (8), Lutheran (2), Presbyterian (1)	
Conservative Protestants	8
including Baptists, Pentecostals, Mennonites, Alliance, Nazarenes	
Other Faith Groups	6
including Jews, Muslims, Buddhists, Hindus, Sikhs	
Religious Nones	16

★A residual 5% or so, mostly Protestants, identify with varied groups that neither fall into these six categories nor collectively represent a family with compatible characteristics.

Data Source: Statistics Canada, 2001 Census.

I use the term "religious families" – versus "denominations" – deliberately. There is undoubtedly a fair amount of movement *between Protestant denominations.* Don Posterski and Irwin Parker reported that, in the mid-1990s, some 40% of highly active Mainline Protestants and

Conservative Protestants said their current denominations represented a switch from the denominations in which they had been raised.[20]

- People who are United, Anglican, Lutheran, and Presbyterian appear to have something of a free trade agreement: they move back and forth to some extent.
- Even more common is the switching between evangelical Protestant groups, where Pentecostal, Baptist, Alliance, Mennonite, Nazarene, and Evangelical Free individuals, for example, move fairly freely between churches.
- Such Protestant switching, particularly in the case of evangelicals, is not necessarily driven by theological factors. It also is not necessarily permanent. While undoubtedly there are times when moves are associated with reluctance, struggle, and strain, they more commonly are the result of fairly prosaic factors such as the choices available in given communities and the attractiveness of a particular church. For such "circulating saints," their next residential move brings the curtain down on what seemed to be a denominational switch.

However, the data show that movement *between religious families* – Mainline Protestants, Conservative Protestants, and Roman Catholics – is quite another thing. It's not that it never happens; it's just that it is relatively rare.[21] For example, our national surveys allowed us to track the affiliation patterns of 363 Canadians over a 20-year period, from 1975 to 1995. What we found was that, during that time, some 95% of Catholics and 85% of Protestants stayed with their religious families. The nation-wide exceptions noted in Chapter 2 were also evident with this sample: (a) the tendency for the offspring of people from Other World Faiths to switch to Christian groups and (b) for a sizable number of Religious Nones to revert to the Catholic and Protestant affiliations of their parents.[22]

Even when some family switching does take place, it's readily apparent that the theological trips are often very short ones. A Conservative Protestant is likely to feel at ease in an Anglican evangelical church. A charismatic Christian is fairly comfortable worshipping in a range of Pentecostal, Catholic, and non-denominational settings where the "gifts of the Spirit" are valued and emphasized. Reciprocally, in the short run at least, a Catholic charismatic may be comfortable worshipping in a non–denominational grassroots Pentecostal church – although the infrequency of the celebration of Eucharist would probably be among the initial unnerving discoveries.

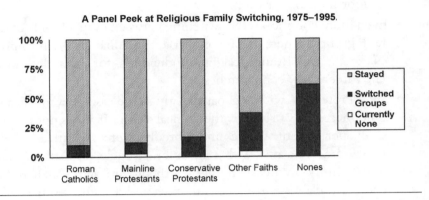

A Panel Peek at Religious Family Switching, 1975–1995.

But, despite these theological and worship affinities, it's also very clear that few charismatic evangelical Protestants think of converting to Catholicism, and vice versa. On the Protestant side, a de-emphasizing of formal church membership has made it possible for people of various religious families to worship together "with no membership strings attached," probably contributing to the illusion that people are freely switching. However, affinities that make for *worship* should not be confused with affinities that make for actual *switching*. A better test of religious identification would be the church of one's choice when one gets married, wants a child baptized, christened, or dedicated, or requires a funeral.

A Renaissance – Along Religious Family Lines

What all of this adds up to is the Canadian religious reality that not all religious groups have equal access to people not actively involved in the churches. To return to the common metaphor, groups have very clear market advantages and disadvantages. Their "market advantage" lies with the people who identify with them: their affiliates. Their "market disadvantage" lies in trying to relate to other groups' affiliates, who variously view them as different and unknown.

Consequently, regardless of the aspirations and resources of any one group that might be committed to "reaching Canada," any such attempts will hit the cement wall of access. In theory, Lutherans and Presbyterians could mount a joint campaign to drop leaflets in every residential mailbox in the country. Pentecostals and Baptists could put a video in every home. Catholics could take a page from the Mormons and Jehovah's Witnesses and knock on every door from coast to coast. Anglicans and the United Church could team up to put together an unprecedented program that puts them on the screen of every computer in the country. And they all could go into mega-debt in the process.

It wouldn't matter. If they are in contact with people who don't identify with them, for the most part the leaflets and videos would be thrown away, the doors would be slammed, and the computer messages would be deleted.

That's why, if a full-blown renaissance of religion is ever going to take place in Canada, it is going to take place along religious group lines. It will involve every group taking responsibility for its own affiliates. Why? Because if they don't, the millions of people who are open to ministry and in need of ministry are going to continue to remain largely unknown to the churches.

- *Roman Catholics*, for example, are in essence called upon to be good stewards of some 13 million Canadians.
- The *United Church of Canada* has three million people who are looking in the direction of that denomination for ministry; in the case of *Anglicans*, the figure is about two million; for the Lutheran and Presbyterian churches, some 500,000 each.
- *Conservative Protestants* have approximately 2.5 million people who, until further notice, are "under their care."

I am fully aware that such segmentation of the Canadian population is not easy for some people to accept – notably for many Conservative Protestants, who are inclined to want to "go after everybody," with the primary goal being evangelism. The problem is that such a strategy is doomed to fail because of the access problem.

(STOP 8.6.05)

Getting Personal and Getting Radical

This leads me to some pointed observations that will be seen as somewhat heretical and potentially unacceptable to some readers. But please hear me out.

It seems to me that if groups experience access problems because of religious self-identification, one obvious solution is for such groups to work together with others that do have access in order to maximize the effectiveness of ministry.

Here's a specific illustration. Dating back to the era of Lower Canada, Protestants have tried to make inroads in Quebec. Yet the Roman Catholic monopoly has remained virtually unchanged through today. In fact, Protestants comprised about 14% of Quebec's population in 1844 and 8% in 1971, but just 4% (250,000 people) today. The attrition is primarily a result of Mainline Protestant losses. The Montreal Anglican Diocese, for example, has seen the number of people on its parish lists drop from 100,000-plus to around 20,000.[23] Conservative Protestants in the province have fared relatively better over the past 160 years, managing to hold a 1–2% "market share." They have been led by Baptists, who numbered 4,063 in 1844 and 36,822 as of 2001 – a net gain of about 33,000 people over a century and a half. During the same period, the number of Catholics has grown from just over 572,000 to almost six million – a gain of close to 5.5 million people.

TABLE 3.4. **Composition of Select Religious Groups in Quebec: 1844–2001**

	1844*	1971	2001
Roman Catholic	82.1%	86.7	83.2
Anglican	6.2	3.0	1.2
United Church	2.3**	2.9	.7
Presbyterian	4.6	.9	.1
Lutheran	.0	.4	.1
Baptist	.6	.6	.5
Pentecostal	—	.2	.3
None	—	1.0	5.6

*Census of Lower Canada. **Methodists

Source: Census of Canada 1870–71, and Statistics Canada, 1971 and 2001 Census Data.

As any Protestant leader working in Quebec knows well, it is tough to grow. I frequently have mentioned the observation of evangelical Edwin Orr in his interesting trek across Canada in the 1930s to assess the religious situation. He wrote that he was told of a Catholic priest who in 1857 turned to evangelical Protestantism and started a work in Quebec City. After 10 years, reported Orr, he had a church of 20 members.[24] Over the years, things have not become much easier for Protestant groups. It is estimated that the 300 or so evangelical congregations in the province have an average Sunday attendance of around 70 people.[25] From time to time we hear about "a Protestant success story," such as the independent Westview Bible Church in Montreal, which has grown from a small congregation to a core of 700 in two decades,[26] or the New Life Church (Église Nouvelle Vie), which has grown from 60 to 2,000 people since being founded in 1993.[27] But such stories are rare.

It therefore seems obvious that a much more effective strategy needs to be pursued by those who aspire to minister in Quebec: work alongside like-minded Roman Catholics. They have something that no other group in the world has: access to Quebec Catholics. If leaders within the Catholic Church in Quebec are willing to work with Mainline and Conservative Protestants, and if Protestants are able to find like-minded Catholics who similarly value Christian faith and are committed to good ministry, it might be possible to make much more effective use of everyone's expertise, energy, and other resources.

Evangelical Protestants, for example, have much to bring. Youth ministry is a particular area of need in Quebec. The same, it seems, can be said of areas such as contemporary worship and small-group ministry – areas in which evangelicals excel. And some of those young evangelical faces with their enthusiasm and vitality wouldn't hurt, either. Working with Catholics rather than going it alone would seem to be a much improved way for Conservative Protestants and others to approach ministry in Quebec.[28]

In April 2002, I had the good fortune to be invited by The Leadership Centre, Willow Creek Canada, to spend a day in Edmonton at a "Prevailing Church Conference" featuring Bill Hybels. As I mentioned earlier, these conferences are held regularly across the county. That day, some 1,200 evangelical church leaders were present; they personified the youth, energy, and growing expertise that are found in much of Conser- ✓

vative Protestant Canada today. Driving back to Lethbridge, I found myself thinking, "What a waste it will be if those kinds of collective resources are limited to nurturing healthy evangelical groups, versus being shared with other religious families that are positioned to reach so many Canadians, but need help."

The same can be said of resources found in the Roman Catholic and Mainline churches. I sometimes think that leaders and laity in individual groups have very little awareness of the wealth of human resources, for example, that exists in our religious families, denominations, and congregations across the country. I often wish that individuals in the various "camps" could meet each other so they could discover that first-hand. On a few occasions, I myself have had the privilege of bringing them together, and smiled at both the surprise and the delight that they experience in the process.

Not Exactly a Given

Yes, I am more than slightly aware that such alliances will not necessarily be easy to come by. It's not just a matter of evangelical Protestants and Quebec Catholics being wary of one another, and also frequently feeling that they are in competition with one another.[29] A major problem among Protestants is the magnitude of the gap between (a) Conservative Protestants and (b) Mainliners generally, and the United Church specifically.[30]

- Our 1994 national survey of the United Church found that ministers were far more likely to say they would feel at home in a native spirituality worship setting (74%) than they would in a Pentecostal service (33%).

- Our 1995 national survey of evangelical Protestant leaders found that, reciprocally, 34% of Pentecostals and 35% of other Conservative Protestants would be equally uncomfortable in a United Church service.

- It's more than denominations being suspicious and even hostile toward each other; such tension and animosity is not uncommon between "conservatives" and "liberals" *within* both Mainline and evangelical denominations. Needless to say, Roman Catholics as well are not always one warm, homogenous, and harmonious body.

Beyond wariness between groups, myriad other issues must be worked through.

- For years I have hammered away at the necessity of cooperative ministry; I still find large numbers of leaders mystified by *why it is necessary*.
- Large numbers of congregations also have a "God bless me and my wife, my brother John and his wife, us four, no more" mentality. They prefer to carry out ministry in a *highly autonomous* way. They aren't about to consider working with other groups.
- Then there is the problem of *competition*. Some churches won't even consider working with those in their own religious families and denominations, let alone groups "on the outside."
- A closely related hurdle is *motivation*. Groups want to know what's in it for them. Many also express concern that it may *cost* them too much.
- Once groups are on board with the collective ministry idea, they still have to clarify what they are able to *bring*.
- Assuming the spirit is willing, many seem to need help in knowing how all of this gets *off the ground*.

Eight Tough Issues Facing the Collective Ministry Ideal
1. **Alienation** – *they are too different from us.*
2. **Comprehension** – *why is it necessary?*
3. **Isolation** – *we prefer to minister by ourselves.*
4. **Competition** – *we can't work with our rivals.*
5. **Motivation** – *why should we bother?*
6. **Debilitation** – *it will take our resources and make us weaker.*
7. **Contribution** – *what do we have to give?*
8. **Initiation** – *how does something like this start?*

But It Has to Happen

It consequently is a major step – indeed, in some instances, an extremely radical step – for groups to consider working more cooperatively and more collectively to ensure that ministry to Canada's millions of affiliates takes place. Nonetheless, it is a step that must be taken – in

Quebec and across the country. If anyone needs a biblical precedent, he or she needs to look no further than the famous Macedonian cry to "come over and help us." As with the disciples of old, it is time for groups to go beyond Jerusalem.

- In some settings, it may mean – as it does in Quebec – groups helping to support a dominant group.
- In many communities across the country, it would translate into leaders of congregations working together in identifying their respective affiliates, and sharing expertise and other resources as they attempt to respond to what they learn about affiliates' interests and needs.

No, I am not calling for groups to abandon their respective distinctions and engage in some kind of lowest-common-denominator type of Christian faith, or, even worse – to borrow theologian and sociologist Gregory Baum's phrase – a collective "pooling of pathologies."[31] On the contrary, what I envision is highly committed and highly competent people aggressively pursuing like-minded spirits in other groups who similarly value faith. As I just indicated, I, like many of you, have spent enough time in enough diverse Christian settings to know that such people exist in every group. What they need to do is find one another – and then explore ways of working together. In time, Canada will feel the difference.

Obviously, the idea of cooperative ministry is not new. National organizations that interact do exist. These include the Canadian Council of Churches, the Canadian Conference of Catholic Bishops, and the Evangelical Fellowship of Canada. Groups frequently have joined together in communities in many parts of Canada to address social issues, deal with catastrophes, hold youth events and study days, carry out Billy Graham–like crusades, do some joint advertising, and so on.[32] Most communities have ministerials that are interdenominational and interfaith in nature. Explicit events such as the Canadian Bible Society (CBS)–initiated *Connexions 2003* are potentially important ventures, especially if they can bring together a wide range of leaders, as this event tried to do. The three-day conference in Toronto in January 2003 was designed to teach Christian executive leaders theory and techniques for developing strategic alliances with one another, a common concept in the corporate world. CBS national director Glen Pitts commented that "a conference of this nature is long overdue," adding that we are "not just here to talk about unity and partnering, but to really begin to forge alliances."[33] There also are indications that dialogue and cooperative efforts are on the rise, between faith groups, and both between and within religious families.[34] Such varied efforts and gatherings show that cooperation is not only possible, but also is productive and highly valued by many.

What I am urging religious groups to do is to make use of their collective resources in pursuing a very specific goal: finding affiliates and, as much as possible, ministering to them.

Of course there will be resistance and indifference to such a collective ministry game plan. But I again remind everyone of the alternative: if groups continue to try to go it alone, they are going to continue to waste a lot of resources. More importantly, they also are going to continue to fail to provide the ministries that Canadians require.

It would seem preferable to attempt to emulate "the Christian body" ideal, and try to do it together. The analogy offered by the Apostle Paul needs to be taken seriously. It's the only way the job is going to get done.

Collective Ministry Through Some Improbable Partnerships

Catholics and Evangelicals need to work together and pray together, David Mainse, the founder of the *100 Huntley Street* national TV show, said recently. Changes are causing Evangelicals, Catholics, and other Christians who agree on the "essential message of Christ, who He is, and why He came," to overcome the barriers keeping them from common action, he said.

Mainse, whose daily Christian TV program has been broadcasting since 1977, shared the hosting duties for many years with a Jesuit priest, Father Bob McDougall. "It threw a lot of people for a loop at the time," he admitted. Bob got a lot of nasty letters from Catholics wondering what he was doing with those Pentecostals, and I got a lot of nasty letters from Evangelicals wondering what I was doing with that Catholic."

Mainse also attributed the warming of relations between Catholics and Evangelicals to factors such as the charismatic renewal, and the papacy of John Paul II. "Again and again he has preached the essentials of the Gospels," said Mainse.

Steve Weatherbe, "Let's Work Together, Says Mainse," Western Catholic Reporter, July 21, 2003.

Five Particular Ministry Challenges

So what do we do if someone calls? The research shows that the affiliates are out there. Many are receptive to greater involvement. However, the key to engaging them lies in being able to provide effective ministry. Here the research findings are clear: religious groups that are serious about attempting to minister to people "on the fringe" face at least five important hurdles. They can be cleared. But they can't be ignored.

1. Spirituality

Canadian religious groups think they have something to say about spirituality. And so they should. Conservative Protestants take considerable pride in the fact that they give premier attention to spirituality. Roman Catholics, Anglicans, and Lutherans likewise place a high level of importance on spirituality, even though its nature and expression may not be quite the same as what many Conservatives have in mind. The United Church has been showing a renewed interest in spirituality in the past decade or so. Presbyterians declared 2003–04 their "Year of Spirituality" as part of their six-part, seven-year *Flames* initiative aimed at enhancing the denomination's ministry.

Our research and that of others makes it very clear that spiritual interests and needs are pervasive among Canadians, including those who are not highly involved in churches.

- Our Project Canada surveys have found that some 75% of adults across the country maintain they have spiritual needs, and a similar proportion has told us that spirituality is important to them.[1]
- Consistent with those results, the 2003 *Time*–Vision TV poll found that 77% of Canadians regard an inner spiritual life as important to them. In addition, six in ten people indicated that they are interested in learning more about religion and spiritual matters.[2]
- Of particular significance, some one in two individuals who either say they have no religion or "never" attend religious services acknowledge both that spirituality is important to them and that they themselves have spiritual needs.[3]

Highly Diverse Meanings

There is a vitally important asterisk, however, to all this. The research shows that when people talk about spirituality, sometimes about all they have in common is the word. Since 1995, we've been asking Canadians what they have in mind when they say they have "spiritual" needs, or when they speak of themselves as being "spiritual."

- We have found that just over half of our respondents are thinking in fairly traditional terms. They talk in terms of "God," "prayer," "a higher power," and so on.
- However, the remaining half offer highly individualistic and subjective ideas of spirituality, including ideas such as "peace of mind," "a feeling of oneness with the earth," "positive thinking," and "inner awareness."
- Significantly, to the extent that people don't *attend* services very often, they also are inclined to hold less conventional views of spirituality. Keep in mind that these individuals, of course, are the very people I've been arguing churches need to reach.
- Less conventional views of spirituality are also more common among *women* than men, as well as among individuals *under 55* versus people who are older.

TABLE 4.1. **Types of Spirituality Responses and Religious and Social Characteristics**

	Conventional Responses	Less Conventional Responses
Nationally	**53%**	47
Weekly	77	23
Monthly	52	48
Yearly	34	66
Never	9	91
Men	62	38
Women	46	54
18–34	48	52
35–54	47	53
55+	71	29

Source: Derived from Bibby, Restless Gods, *2004:197.*

These findings serve as a very important reminder that the term "spirituality" embraces extremely diverse ideas.[4] Religious groups that value spirituality need to ask themselves a very blunt question: do they currently have much to offer people who do not conceptualize spirituality in the same way that they do?

It is not uncommon for evangelicals, for example, to think they are better prepared than many other groups to speak to spiritual needs. Presbyterians, in their "Year of Spirituality," claimed to be "seeking to engage the church in an ongoing discussion on the breadth and depth of the topic of Spirituality." Yet the breadth, at least, had built-in parameters: "The church will be guided by its understanding of Spirituality as our continuing response to the reality of God's grace in Jesus Christ, through the work of the Holy Spirit."[5]

Unfortunately, that's not exactly what half the nation has in mind. Ironically, any group – Presbyterian, Conservative Protestant, or otherwise – that assumes it has something to say about spirituality just because it places a high value on spirituality may in fact have little to say to millions of Canadians. They are not talking about the same thing. In the words of Calgary's Roman Catholic Bishop, Fred Henry, "Many of the beliefs and practices in these constructed spiritualities are purely private." He adds, "I have been invited to many 'retreats,' even to be a presenter at such experiences, and left with the feeling that it was a nice get-together but God was either not invited or declined to attend."[6]

Churches have to find ways of putting the diverse spirituality pieces together. The prognosis, however, is not particularly good. One reason is that Christians themselves don't have a high level of consensus on what constitutes spirituality. Harsh though it may sound, it's apparent to any serious onlooker that they are far from being in agreement when it comes to basic Christology – an important key to understanding why cooperative ministry is frequently so difficult to achieve.

Take the diverse reactions to Mel Gibson's 2004 box office record-breaker, *The Passion of the Christ*.

- On the one extreme, a two-year-old Southern Baptist church in Oakville, Ontario, The Sanctuary, purchased 4,000 tickets at an estimated cost of $60,000 and offered them free to the public. Pastor Jeff Christopherson claimed, "For a Christian, it revitalizes your understanding of what the cross is all about."[7] Campus Crusade, with help from Outreach Canada, Alpha Canada, Focus on the Family, Christian Direction, Catholic Evangelization Training Ministries and the Evangelical Fellowship of Canada, took a rough cut of the film on a cross-country tour in January 2004, showing it to an estimated 9,000 pastors and ministry leaders in nine cities over six days. The screenings, said the organizers, were held to encourage Christians to use the film to reach out to their non-Christian friends and neighbours.[8]

- On the other extreme, an editorial in *Catholic New Times* said the film reflects a literalist and premodern world view, "not only of its creator, Mel Gibson, who is an ultra-traditionalist Catholic, but of scripture itself." Such a literalistic framework, while appealing to "fundamentalists and their moviemakers," according to the editorial, has "no purchasing power for people of the enlightenment today." The writer is "saddened by the genuine distress of readers not yet brought up-to-date as might have been expected," adding, "Atonement as one bloody death on the cross has little to say to modern people about how one man's death two thousand years ago affects us today."[9]

Yet, perhaps in the strange ways that God works in life, the very diversity of meanings that exist among Canada's religious groups when it comes to faith and spirituality may turn out to be a strength. That diversity may be essential to responding to the remarkably varied meanings that are characterizing Canadians who are pursuing spiritual quest.

What People Mean by "Spiritual" When They Speak of Spiritual Needs

Conventional

"...living in fellowship with Christ...believing in God and the Bible...that God is there for us, hears our prayers and answers them...need to know there is a power greater than me...need God's spirit to guide, protect and support me in good times and bad...building a personal relation with Jesus Christ...nourishing our souls so we can be closer to God...the need to reconnect with my religion...the need for strength, comfort, and courage available from a power beyond ourselves... to be a good Christian...something greater than me or mankind...to pray and commune with my heavenly Father...a devotion to things of God and not material things...Christianity...a belief in a presence beyond our bodily beings... a loving God...knowing there is a God and a guardian angel that looks after us... the need to attend mass more often..."

Less Conventional

"...a matter relating to our inner-self or soul...peace of mind...a feeling of oneness with the earth and with all that is within me...the existence of an immortal soul that has to be cared for...our relationship with God or nature or the universe...positive thinking and excitement...can be religious or the beauty of nature of the love of family and friends... a feeling that a force controls the universe...the human spirit and goodness of humankind that ultimately triumphs over evil...searching for meaning...a deeper appreciation and understanding of myself, others, and God...recognition and nurturing the needs of the soul...a feeling of being whole and at peace with my experiences in life...inner awareness...belief that somehow there is some influencing force...my presence and communication with the world around me...feeling there is something more to life than the obvious here and now..."

Source: Adapted from Bibby, Restless Gods, *2004:198.*

Where Spirituality is Shared

Our research has also uncovered another sobering finding: remarkably few "church-going" Canadians are sharing their spirituality with people in their own religious settings. Asked directly, about half say, "I keep my spirituality pretty much to myself." One third indicate that they share it with "some people who are close to me, outside of religious groups." Only 12% report that they can relate their spirituality "to others in my religious group." The latter include less than one in three actively involved, weekly attenders.[10]

Spirituality is a highly diverse, elusive, and private phenomenon. Consequently, the official conceptions of spirituality that religious groups have may be very different, not only from what average Canadians have in mind, but also from what their own actively involved people have in mind.[11] Maybe, in some instances, the problem lies in not providing the right of kind of opportunities and environments for their actively involved people – let alone others – to reflect on spirituality.

At a minimum, these findings point to the need for churches that believe they have something to bring to conversations about spirituality to develop creative ways of opening up the communication lines on spirituality – beginning with their own people and then moving outward.[12] In the process, they won't lack competition. Michael Higgins and Douglas Letson note that while the thirst for a meaningful or living spirituality is unquenchable, "there are not a few purveyors of the 'spiritual arts' willing to peddle their dubious wares at a speedy rate and at cut-rate costs."[13] They maintain that a spirituality that is communal, historical, theological, with justice as part of its very definition, is a spirituality best poised to thrive in the new century.[14] Maybe it's not what most Canadians have in mind; maybe it can be.

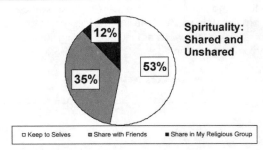

Source: Bibby, Restless Gods, *2004:201.*

2. Personal and Relational Needs

A second particularly important challenge for ministry has to do with the ability of congregations to contribute to individuals and their relationships.

Lots of People Could Use Some Help

The research documents what all of us know well. People not only want to stay alive, they also want to live well. We Canadians value relationships above everything else, while also placing a lot of importance on freedom, a comfortable life, success and careers.

But we also are well aware that, while life brings a lot of pleasure, it also brings a lot of pain and strain. To varying degrees, we find ourselves concerned about a range of issues: relationships and children, money and time, school and jobs, health and aging, people dying.[15]

Take relationships. Yes, it's true that nothing is more important to Canadians, young and old, than good ties with other people. However, we are well aware that all is not always great on the relational front.

- Personal and intimate relationships are frequently accompanied by anxiety and grief.
- Despite the fact that both teens and parents place supreme value on friendship and love, both too often experience conflict with and alienation from one another.
- Frequently, people have less than great interpersonal ties at work, at school, and in communities – and sometimes, can you believe, even at church.
- Interpersonal life obviously could be much improved at other levels: regionally, nationally, and globally. An April 2004 cover story in *Maclean's*, for example, decried the pervasiveness of rudeness in Canadian life. "After an intellectual enlightenment, a couple of world wars and a communications revolution, you'd think we'd made a few strides in the realm of daily human relations," wrote Charlie Gillis. "But in the last couple of decades, all the available evidence suggests the opposite has taken place. If anything, we appear to be losing ground."[16]

On Being the Salt of the Earth

The church here understands itself as an agent of justice and peace. I belong to a small committee set up by the Quebec bishops to study the church's response to the new cultural and religious pluralism in society. We discussed the difficult question of how the church's mission to proclaim the gospel can be reconciled with its mission to promote justice, peace and reconciliation. One participant said that he did not find this difficult at all. When Jesus said, "You are the salt of the earth," he indicated that the church was to remain a minority in the human family. Salt is present in small quantities. If everyone became "salt," humanity would become an inedible salt cake.

Gregory Baum, "New Understanding of Mission," Catholic New Times, *May 5, 2002.*

Religious groups presumably have much to bring in enhancing personal life. The Christian faith has a great deal to say about how people can experience optimum relationships. The faith also speaks of a God and Christian communities that can help provide resources for people who are struggling with life, including offering them hope in the face of failings, struggles, and, of course, death. It also is a faith that calls for social justice that makes enriched living possible.

Currently, churches are not coming out all that high as an explicit, direct resource for most Canadians during times of personal need. Given a chance to cite two major sources of help when they are facing serious problems, a solid majority say they turn to family members, and some say they look to friends or to God and prayer. Only a very small number typically rely on specialists, with clergy cited by less than 1%. About one in ten find that in tough times they rely primarily on themselves, sometimes because of choice, sometimes because of necessity.

Clearly, large numbers of people could use more help in dealing with life. On the surface, religious groups seem well positioned to contribute.

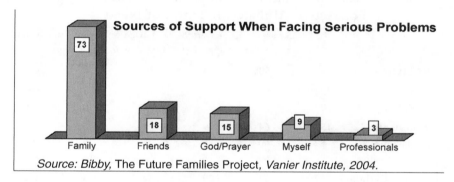

Sources of Support When Facing Serious Problems

Family	Friends	God/Prayer	Myself	Professionals
73	18	15	9	3

Source: Bibby, The Future Families Project, *Vanier Institute, 2004.*

Two Hurdles

However, groups that aspire to minister better to the personal needs of their less active affiliates face two challenges. *First*, they must *be aware* of such needs. *Second*, they must *be able to respond* to what they find.

The latter challenge is a complex one that I want to deal with in detail in the next two chapters. The awareness hurdle is one that can be seen in the responses to a national survey question I posed in 2000. We asked people who currently attend services at least once a month (1) how aware religious groups have been of their personal problems over the years, and (2) how much support the groups have provided.

- What we found was that, contrary to the lament we sometimes hear about groups not being willing to be there for people, only 7% reported that groups *failed to give them the support they needed when the groups were aware* of what they were going through.

- Another 50% told us that groups generally were *aware of their problems and came through* with appropriate support. They were led by weekly versus monthly attenders.
- However, what was disturbing was to learn that the remaining 43% said their religious groups *were not aware* of their personal problems — although almost half of these same people said they nonetheless found help from the groups in dealing with their difficulties. Presumably they found nurture in services, social ties, and the like.

TABLE 4.2. **Role of Religious Groups in Providing Support For Active Affiliates in Times of Need**

	N	Aware & Supported	Unaware & Supported	Unaware & Not Given	Aware But Not Given	Totals
NATIONALLY	287	**50%**	**23**	**20**	**7**	**100**
Weekly	204	56	22	16	6	100
Monthly	82	37	25	32	6	100
Protestants	157	**64**	**19**	**9**	**8**	**100**
Mainline	82	60	26	8	6	100
Conservative	46	59	13	13	15	100
Roman Catholics	117	**32**	**29**	**34**	**5**	**100**
Quebec	41	34	27	32	7	100
Outside Quebec	76	32	30	34	4	100

Source: Bibby, Restless Gods, *2002:208.*

What is particularly noteworthy are the differences reported by Roman Catholics and Protestants.

- While 72% of *Protestants* said their churches were aware of their problems, the awareness figure in the case of Catholics was only 37%.
- This means that more than six in ten *Catholics* indicated that their parishes were unaware of their personal problems, as did close to three in ten Protestants.

- Although the sample sizes are small and the results therefore preliminary, the findings suggest that awareness of problems is somewhat higher among Conservative Protestants (74%) than their Mainline counterparts (66%).

The Protestant figures show that much more needs to be done; three in ten people overall translates into about 2.5 million monthly-plus attenders. But the Catholic figure of more than six in ten points to a serious problem. It may lie, among other things, in the size of parishes and in the lack of opportunities for interaction where personal matters might be able to surface, such as social gatherings or small-group activities.

An extremely important implication here is this: if so many Catholic and Protestant churches are unaware of the personal concerns of their frequent attenders, what are the chances that they will be aware of the personal needs of relatively inactive affiliates – let alone respond to such needs?

We all know that there are some issues we prefer to keep to ourselves. We also have just seen that many people who face serious problems prefer to turn to family members. That could be one reason why churches often are not aware of difficulties individuals are encountering. However, the pronounced Catholic and Protestant differences suggest there is more involved than just issues of privacy and family resources. Groups simply are frequently oblivious to the pressing problems faced by people sitting in their pews.

It's not the way things are supposed to be. In describing a mature and fully developed Christian life, the Catholic Church's *General Directory for Catechesis* maintains, "As the vitality of the human body depends on the proper function of all of its organs, so also the maturation of the Christian life requires that it be cultivated in all its dimensions: knowledge of the faith, liturgical life, moral formation, prayer, belonging to community, missionary spirit."[17] "Belonging to community" does not simply mean worship and learning together. "Apart from its didactic aspect, the Christian group is called to be an experience of community."[18] Moreover, "The parish is called to be a fraternal and welcoming family where Christians become aware of being the people of God."[19] Such ideals are hardly realized when member individuals are oblivious to each other's pain.

Given the size of many of their parishes, perhaps more Catholic churches need to do what many Protestant congregations frequently do: provide opportunities for people with similar interests and needs to meet in small groups. Such are the sentiments of Waterloo, Ontario, priest Frank Ruetz, who maintains there is a hunger for "Small Christian Communities" and has been spreading the news to the rest of the country. He has developed opportunities for groups to share faith through Scripture readings, study, and reflection that are aimed at helping them connect their life experiences to the readings. "This is a heart phenomenon," he says, adding, "There is a hunger for the kind of faith community created in these groups." Father Ruetz goes so far as to say that he thinks the church can be renewed and revitalized by these kinds of Small Christian Communities.[20]

As with spirituality, improved ministry to the personal needs of affiliates needs to start with those who are involved, and then move outward. Until then, groups will have little to offer their marginal and inactive affiliates, as well as their disaffiliates.

3. Youth

Everyone recognizes the importance of having young people involved in their groups. What is less obvious is what can be done to stimulate their interest, see them embrace Christian faith, and have them work alongside adults of all ages in ministry.[21] There is not an awful lot of room for error. Viability – present and future – requires that young people be part of churches.

We've been doing a fair amount of research on Canadian youth over the past two decades. Don Posterski and I carried out comprehensive national surveys of young people between the ages of 15 and 19 in 1984 and 1992. I rounded out the project with a further national youth survey in 2000.[22]

Significant Interest in Spirituality – and Religion

Here are some quick, pertinent findings. For starters, contrary to popular thinking, large numbers of young people are interested in both spirituality and religion. The "teenage market" is extensive.

- Our research, and that of others, shows that young people are fascinated with the *supernatural realm*, and hold traditional *beliefs* on levels comparable to adults.
- As we saw earlier, large numbers believe they have *experienced* the presence of *God*. Their openness to mystery is further suggested by the finding that even larger numbers feel they have *experienced precognition*.
- *Religious identification* is high (76%), and – surprising to just about everyone – the proportion of teens *attending services* on a regular weekly basis has been almost identical to adults. About 1 in 5 teens say they have been receiving high levels of *enjoyment* from involvement in religious groups, the same proportion as adults.

TABLE 4.3. **Beliefs, Involvement, and Spirituality: Adults and Teens**

	ADULTS	TEENS
Beliefs		
God exists	81%	73
God or a higher power cares about me	73	68
In life after death	68	78
In ESP	66	59
Experience		
Have personally experienced precognition	58	63
Have felt presence of God/higher power	47	36
Group Involvement		
Identify with a group	86	76
Attend weekly	21	22
Less than monthly; open greater involvement	55	39
Receive high enjoyment from group	22	21
Spirituality		
Have spiritual needs	73	48
Spirituality is important to me★	70	60
Pray privately weekly or more	47	33

Source: Bibby, Canada's Teens, *2001:252, 254, and ★Project Canada Surveys.*

- Approximately 1 in 2 young people acknowledge that they have *spiritual needs,* and more than half say that *spirituality is important* to them. Two in three report that they *pray privately,* one in three at least once a week.
- And, in the face of widespread perception, the real shocker? About 40% who attend services less than once a month nonetheless say that they are *receptive to greater involvement* with religious groups *if* they found it to be worthwhile.

What It Will Take

The youth research also provides some important clues about what is required for young people to become involved. The surveys have found that there is nothing more important to teens than their *friends.* In all three surveys, friendship has topped the value rankings and also has been at the top of the charts when we have asked them what they enjoy most. Number two on the enjoyment list has been *music.* Number two on the value list has been *freedom.*

TABLE 4.4. **Teens' Top 5 Values and Enjoyment Sources**			
	NATIONALLY	**MALES**	**FEMALES**
Values: "Very Important"			
Friendships	85%	80	90
Freedom	85	84	85
Being loved	77	65	87
Having choices	76	73	79
A comfortable life	73	71	74
Enjoy: "A Great Deal"/"Quite A Bit"			
Friends	94	93	95
Music	90	87	92
Your own room	75	67	82
Your mother	71	65	76
Dating	69	70	68

Source: Bibby, Canada's Teens, *2001:13, 24.*

It's a pretty modest creative jump to deduce that, if the three most important features of teenage life are friendship, music, and freedom, young people can be expected to be receptive to environments where all three are found.

- To the extent that religious groups are sensitive to the value teens place on *friends* and friendship, they obviously should be creating environments where friends can be with friends, where there are lots of opportunities for friends to interact with each other. In the wise words of my colleague Posterski, what young people invariably want to know is not "What's taking place?" but rather "Who's going to be there?"

- Since *music* is second only to friends as a source of enjoyment for teens, it's important that music – and the kinds of music *they* like – be present wherever possible. How do older people like us determine what music is appropriate? We don't. Let young people decide for themselves.

- This brings us to a third important feature of environments where teenagers will want to be: *freedom*. They want the freedom to be and to think. These are the years when children are turning into adults. They are experiencing multi-dimensional development: physically, sexually, socially, culturally, emotionally, intellectually, spiritually. They need a lot of room to emerge.[23] The research is clear: during their teen years, young people enjoy individuals and organizations that can find a balance between giving them room and giving them a measure of direction. It's not a new guideline. When we had a parent or a teacher or a counsellor or a coach who succeeded in finding that balance, we enjoyed them. The same was true of organizations. Then, as now, young people enjoy environments where they can be themselves. In religious settings, that means they have to have the opportunity to express their thoughts, including their doubts and embryonic heresies. They need to be free to ask pointed questions about sex. They have to be able to openly discuss faith and life, without feeling the script has already been written by paternalist adults who know how the story has to end. And they have to be able to feel comfortable with how they dress and look.

Friendships, music, freedom: those are the basic features of environments that young people enjoy. In the case of religious groups, two other features need to be added.

The first is *authenticity*; the second is *significance*. In their important book on youth ministry, *Soul Searching the Millennial Generation*, Dave Overholt and James Penner emphasize the need for authenticity in dealing with young people. They remind readers that "adolescents pick up the scent of pretenders" via "BS detectors [that] are always on." For example, they warn those who would use technology to attract youth that "gimmicks do not entice young people," citing one young person who confided, "You win people with content. Cheesy gimmicks only hurt your message."

TABLE 4.5. **Enjoyment Teens Receive from Their Religious Groups**	
% Indicating Receive "A Great Deal" or "Quite a Bit" of Enjoyment	
Nationally	21%
Roman Catholic	20
Outside Quebec	22
Quebec	17
Protestant	41
Mainline	19
United	15
Anglican	17
Conservative	56
Baptist	49
Pentecostal	62
Other Faiths	35

Source: Bibby, Project Teen Canada 2000.

Part of that authentic content, they maintain, involves religious leaders being direct about God and faith. After all, we have documented that young people have religious and spiritual interests and needs. Overholt and Penner note, "In years past, some youth workers thought that not talking of God in their church meetings would make teens more comfortable coming to them. Teens *want* to talk about God" and "explore the questions of the ages."[24] They expect it of churches. Atmospheres characterized by the presence of friends and music and freedom also need to be places where spirituality is explored, people challenged, commitments made, and faith deepened.

Finally, as with adults, if young people are going to bother with church, the key in the long run is for them to find that their involvement is worth their time – that religion significantly touches and enhances their lives. Other factors may bring them in; significance will keep them in.

In the mid-1990s, the former head of the Canadian Conference of Catholic Bishops, Marcel Gervais, made a significant observation: "I am convinced that the future of the Church lies with youth ministry."[25] As noted in Chapter 1, the increase in the participation of young people in the past decade appears to be in large part due precisely to the intentional efforts of a growing number of groups to intensify youth ministry. What they are finding is the same thing that we are finding with adults: the "demand" is there and undoubtedly has been there all along. What is different is that the "suppliers" are finally doing a better job of coming through.

However, good youth ministry is still far from complete. Groups are moving at different speeds and numerical inroads are barely beginning to show. In addition, children and youth ministry is an activity that never ends. Babies keep arriving. Still further, the research shows that millions of the children and teenagers of uninvolved affiliates are at this point being only superficially touched by youth ministries.

Reaching young people – especially those whose parents are among the less involved affiliates – will continue to be one of the greatest challenges facing churches into the foreseeable future.

4. Worship and Music

A fourth important hurdle facing churches is how to provide worship and music that can be meaningful for both active and less active affiliates of all ages. It is a particularly important issue in ministering to people on the fringes of church life since, for many, a service is a primary point of contact.

Probably soon after the first gatherings of Christians, people disagreed on what constituted meaningful worship, with tension between being structured and being extemporaneous. In a sermon delivered in 2004 at a U.S.-Canadian gathering of bishops, Raymond Schultz, the National Bishop of the Evangelical Lutheran Church in Canada, put things this way:

> As the centuries progressed and the Roman forum became the model for church architecture, Roman contract law became the model for ecclesiology. Instead of being unconditionally moved by the Spirit, people now responded to the liturgy with the contractual phrase, "Yes, by the help of God." Instead of kissing each other, they kissed an icon that the priest handed around, then they finally quit kissing altogether and the practice degenerated into the desultory hand shaking that we do today at the passing of the peace. How's that for closing the door on...the Spirit?[26]

In a revealing analysis of recent Canadian national survey findings, Posterski and his associates have claimed that there are four dominant "spiritual styles" among monthly-plus attenders that reflect themselves in worship preferences and needs.[27] About half either are *tolerant* of what people find meaningful (35%) or seem *divergent* in resonating with some parts of services but not others (20%). The others have more identifiable leanings that are either *charismatic* (30%) or *traditional* (15%) in nature. These styles, they maintain, are found everywhere. It can result in "a worship war." Significantly, one place they see the diverse worshippers coming together is at the communion table.

Undoubtedly for much of their history, Canada's Protestant and Catholic groups have felt the need to update their worship services, including music, to ensure that they are meaningful to their people. However, perhaps because of the speed of social and cultural change, perhaps because of a heightened sense of the urgency of making worship relevant, those changes appear to have accelerated since the 1960s.

- Canadian Roman Catholics, in response to Vatican II (1962–65) and the call for modernization of the Church, began to experience mass in their own languages, rather than Latin, with the priest now facing them. A renewed emphasis was placed on preaching and the interpretation of Scripture, along with congregational singing. A new emphasis was placed on lay participation in the services.

- Anglicans, after centuries of dependence on the *Book of Common Prayer* (BCP), were offered an updated liturgy option with the approval of the *Book of Alternative Services* (BAS) in 1983. They still had the freedom to use the BCP; the BAS became a permitted but not required alternative.[28] The Anglicans' 1938 hymnal was also updated in 1971.

- In the United Church, a new book, *Songs for a Gospel People*, became available in 1987 as a supplement to the denomination's standard hymnal of 1971, which had been jointly produced with the Anglicans; the latter, reflecting more cautious times, had carried the title *The Hymn Book*.

- Evangelicals, of course, are not a homogenous group. Still, fairly pervasive buzzwords such as "relevancy" and concepts such as "translating the gospel into modern terms" saw many evangelical churches in the 1960s and onward move away from the use of the King James Version of the Bible, and in the process abandon its language of "thee's" and "thou's" in services. Old hymns that spoke of "lighthouses" and "rock" were frequently discarded in favour of new songs with fresh and more familiar imagery. Organs and pianos were increasingly supplemented with guitars, drums, keyboards, and other instruments. In addition, the charismatic movement was influencing the way in which worship was being expressed in a growing number of places.

Describing worship changes that began to emerge in the late 1970s and 1980s, historian George Webster Grant summed up Canadian developments this way:

> Services in many churches became more informal, participative, and popular, sometimes chatty, and occasionally gimmicky. The "kiss of peace," a primitive practice revived in the 1960s, became in many congregations an interlude of vigorous handshaking, and in some cases, as an unsympathetic observer commented, of "hugging, touching, and kissing." Celebration replaced reverence as the ideal of liturgical reforms, introducing displays of banners, flourishes of trumpets, and a revival of liturgical dance.[29]

The Powerful Place of Music in Christian Lives

It was one of those insightful mistakes. The workshop leader had two burgundy-coloured books on the table in front of him. Without looking down, he selected one of the books, held it up before the group, and said, "This is the church's first and most essential resource for the nurturing of faith." The puzzled looks on the faces of the people prompted him to glance at what he was holding. It was *Voices United*. He had intended to pick up the Bible. "Whoops," he said. "Let me try that again." What he wanted to point out was that *next* to the Bible, a hymn book is a congregation's most important resource for the nurture and development of faith. For some in the gathering, it was no mistake. Hymns were indeed central to their growth in faith and discipleship, in some ways more directly influential than scripture.

John E. Ambrose (1997), minister and managing editor of the United Church hymn and worship resource Voices United, *1996.*

The Current Escalation

The changes that Grant had been witnessing in worship and music appear to have increased considerably through the 1990s and into the early years of our new century.

- Praise and Worship songs, primarily imported from the U.S. and available on discs and – as necessary – on overheads, are now widely used, particularly in Protestant churches.

- Drama and dance have been incorporated into worship services in what appears to be a sizable number of settings.

- Roman Catholic services have tended to become somewhat less formal, with more emphasis on congregational involvement, including singing. Once bound to the liturgies of Europe, parishes are able to benefit from a dramatic upsurge in the number of new hymns being written by Catholics.[30]

- In 1996, the United Church released a new hymn and worship book entitled *Voices United*; it was supplemented in 1999 by a "prayer and praise" book, *Spirit Anew*. Some congregations are drawing on what is known as the Ancient Culture movement, mixing together mystery, sacrament, wonder, and ancient styles of worship and music in contemporary formats. In some settings, worship draws on diverse sources, such as Native spirituality, Celtic Christianity, and the Taizé Catholic community in France.[31] Labyrinths have known a rise in popularity.[32] There also is no lack of experimentation with praise bands, drama, screens, and PowerPoint.[33]

- The Anglican Church of Canada updated its 1971 hymnbook in 1998 with a new hymnal, *Common Praise*. It also has witnessed growing diversity in worship forms across the denomination. Indicative of that diversity, a 2003 national committee initiated a research project exploring the degree of latitude that exists in using new texts, and the prevalence and impact of features including new music, worship arts, "visual treasures," liturgical dance, and drama.[34]

- In 1991, the General Assembly of the Presbyterian Church in Canada authorized *The Book of Common Worship* for voluntary use as a worship resource book. It was the product of 11 years of research and testing. In 1997 a new hymnal, *The Book of Praise*, was released that had been in the making for six years and served as an update to its 1972 predecessor.[35] It is interesting to see that at a recent national Assembly gathering, a report from the young adult representatives called for more youth-run services, participation of youth in worship planning, the use of new instruments, and the inclusion of new forms of worship.[36]

- In 2001, the Evangelical Lutheran Church in Canada (ELCIC) embarked on a major five-year *Renewing Worship* project in collaboration with the Evangelical Lutheran Church in America, aimed at renewing worship and creating resources to succeed the 1978 *Lutheran Book of Worship*. In explaining the need for change, the ELCIC pointed out to its constituents that "the pace of change within the church and beyond has quickened," citing features including greater ecumenism, broader understandings of culture, increased musical diversity, and changes in language use. Such developments have affected the expression of "word and sacrament," calling for a renewal of worship and resources that is grounded in the past while open to the future.[37]

Such changes have been only the tip of what American congregational expert Lyle Schaller has described as a major transformation of worship. Schaller says it is characterized by "the arrival of a new era in church music" and "the change in public worship" in thousands of churches "from a dull and boring weekly obligation to an appealing and exciting worship experience."[38]

Generally speaking, Conservative Protestants perhaps have been willing to be the most innovative, widely adopting so-called contemporary worship and music, complete with worship-team bands of five to seven people who typically are 40 years old or younger. Guitars, keyboards, and drums are featured. Mind you, some greying Pentecostals can be forgiven for asking what's so new about all this? They were doing those kinds of things back in the 1950s!

Evangelicals have further led the way in overhauling older sanctuaries and building new ones that feature stage-like platforms and chairs rather than pews. Hymnals have either been discarded or are seldom used in favour of overhead and PowerPoint presentations of the words to the music being sung. Those present are encouraged to be both spontaneous and individualistic as they worship, frequently raising hands, clapping hands, closing eyes, murmuring words, standing up — and in some settings, dancing in the aisles. Traditional sermons are frequently presented in a fairly informal manner, with the assistance of PowerPoint and other multi-media resources. These are not the kind of services and settings that Grandma and most of her children grew up with.

We wanted to get a reading on the prevalence of contemporary versus traditional worship services. Therefore, in our 2000 national survey we asked Canadians who attend worship services at least once a month to describe the nature of their worship services.

- Just one in three indicated that their services are *traditional*.
- The most common response — offered by close to half the respondents — was that their services are *a blend* of traditional and contemporary worship forms. Relatively few said that their services are *contemporary* or that their churches have separate services that feature *both forms*.
- Catholics living outside Quebec were the most likely to report that their services are traditional in nature (47%) in contrast to Conservative Protestants, who were the least to do so (17%). About five in ten Quebec Catholics and Mainline Protestants said their services are a blend of both styles. Evangelicals were more likely than others (21%) to report having only contemporary services.

TABLE 4.6. **Types of Worship Services by Religion Family**

	Traditional	Contemporary	Blend of Both	Both in Sep Services	Unsure	Totals
Nationally	36%	8	45	6	5	100
RC Outside Quebec	47	4	36	9	4	100
RC: Quebec	33	10	50	0	7	100
Mainline Protestant	29	3	56	9	3	100
Conservative Protestant	17	21	45	7	10	100

Source: Bibby, Project Canada 2000.

Obviously, the terms "traditional" and "contemporary" are highly relative. Nonetheless, the general patterns seem fairly clear. Evangelicals are doing the most experimenting with contemporary worship. However, efforts to at least supplement traditional styles of worship are also common in Mainline Protestant and Quebec Catholic churches. Contemporary worship is somewhat less prevalent in Catholic services in the rest of the country, but still is found in approximately one in two parishes.

Incidentally, it is interesting to see that a comparison of worship styles in Canada and the United States among Protestant churches suggests that, if anything, Canadians are somewhat more willing to opt for contemporary worship forms than Americans. U.S. churches are slightly more likely than ours to favour traditional styles and to be less inclined to go solo with contemporary forms of worship.[39]

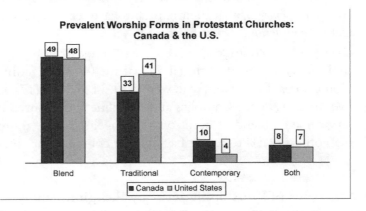

New Worship and New Music: Not for Everyone

As every reader undoubtedly knows well, the acceleration of so-called contemporary services and contemporary music in the last two decades or so has not always been greeted with enthusiasm.[40] Anglican Bishop Anthony Burton has reminded us that such disagreements are not new. "Liturgical dispute," he says, "has a long history," as do "theological disputes fought on the battlefield of liturgy."[41] Worship and music are obviously intertwined. To mess with one's music is to mess with one's worship. The importance that people give to music can be seen in the fact that changes have resulted in considerable conflict and division, particularly in Protestant congregations. Some dissenters have left for other congregations; in some instances major church splits have occurred.

At a gathering of about 20 North American congregational researchers and practitioners in Louisville, Kentucky, in summer 2000, the dominant opinion was that church music is the number one source of congregational division in Protestant churches today – readily outdistancing such issues as sexual orientation.[42] Roman Catholic parishes also have been far from unanimous in their acceptance of post–Vatican II liturgy, lay leadership in services, greater informality, and newer kinds of music – especially when that music has been accompanied in the sanctuary by Protestant-like overhead screens and PowerPoint-producing computers.

For the sociologist looking on, the practical question that comes out of all this activity and controversy concerning worship and music is this: How well are people served – how well are they ministered to? Put another way, to whom is the music being marketed? Who is the target group?

A Critical Take on Contemporary Music

What's hot and what's not nowadays in the church? Music can serve as one example – a very important example for almost every churchgoer. What's hot – at least in some churches – are electric guitars, synthesizers, and vocalists backing up Scripture songs and choruses. What's not are pipe organs or pianos accompanying hymns. Is there anything wrong with that?

What's wrong with that is what's wrong with – or at least limited about – pop music in general. Except for the very best, it generally hits you hard with a shot of pleasure, and then it leaves you physically and emotionally stimulated but intellectually and spiritually malnourished. Most of it is junk food: You don't need teeth to eat it, and there is nothing to digest. The moronic, "Baby, baby, love, love" of MTV gets baptized into "Jesus, Jesus, love, love" with approximately the same effect: warm fuzzies.

Now, I welcome my share of warm fuzzies, and I like a wide range of popular music. But Christians are not growing when their worship music is restricted to five-chord pop tunes, endlessly repeated choruses and lyrics that – at best – contain interchangeable bits of Scripture with no obvious progression of thought. "Precious Jesus, Rock of Ages/Holy Great I Am/Friend of Sinners, Our Messiah/ Worthy Is the Lamb" – oh dear! (I would now warn readers that this impressive lyric of my very own composition – indeed, composed right here on the spot – is protected by copyright *if* I believe that one could actually remember it for more than two minutes).

There is more to Christ and the Christian life than such simplicities, no matter how sincerely expressed, and other music, other worship styles in general, are needed to express this "more."

Professor John G. Stackhouse, Jr. of Regent College, Vancouver in Evangelical Landscapes (Grand Rapids: Baker 2003:16).

Years ago as a seminary student, I listened with considerable interest when a rural Baptist student, literally from the hills of Kentucky, asked our music professor, "Professor Heeren, what is good church music?" I thought, wow, is he going to get it! The professor was an articulate, bright, and seasoned musician. His personal preference seemed to be fairly formal, classical-like church music played on the seminary's mammoth pipe organ, which at the time was allegedly the largest in the American south. Professor Heeren didn't hesitate for a moment: "Good music," he said, "is music that has meaning for that congregation."

I never forgot that. Appropriate music is not my call or yours. It is music that is aimed at someone, and hits home.

It seems to me that what's most important in the current debate and occasional warfare about music and worship is that churches make sure the music they choose hits home. Particularly when I am writing books like this one, I make an extra point of trying to visit as many diverse churches as possible to see what they are doing in the way of worship. My recurring sense is that in so many situations, what's taking place seldom hits home – not merely with me, but with others.

- Sometimes it seems to be because the person leading the services simply wants to get through the liturgy and get to the Eucharist and get people out the doors. Who cares if people in the pews give every indication that they are bored spectators? It makes me long for something new.

- On other occasions, I see a worship band on a platform with their eyes closed from the time they start, seemingly caught up in instant sanctimony, acting intense and emotional. They seem to be religious performers who are unaware that most of their audience is not sharing their sanctimonious seriousness. Presumably this is not a time for much interaction. It makes me long for something older.

- And then I look around at the people in the services, wondering who the music is aimed at. If the music is aimed at God, well, then maybe it starts to make more sense. But if the music is aimed at people sharing in something that is aimed at God, the project is floundering badly.

- I am particularly intrigued to frequently hear that the service is aimed primarily at "seekers," "searchers" – or, to use the term United Church minister Gordon Turner prefers, "drifters." But the sociologist in me wonders, "How many of those kinds of people are actually here?"

- Another common explanation is that the music and worship are aimed at young people. That's why so many older people like my aging mom tried – unsuccessfully, for the most part – to endure what she dubbed "that new stuff." But here again, I have my doubts. I look over at the section in the church that is filled predominantly with the young people the rest of the church seems to be "subsidizing," and I don't see a high level of interest or enthusiasm there either. Then again, our surveys have been telling us that Canadian teens in recent years have been enjoying the likes of the Backstreet Boys, Blink-182, DMX, and Eminem. As far as I can tell, this "contemporary" church music doesn't sound like the music I hear as I flip past MuchMusic on my way to the sports channel. Where did you say it came from? By the way, a lot of active members are paying quite a price for such precarious thinking – if they bother to stay. As I playfully suggested a few years back to the music minister in my mother's church, who knows me and my best intentions well, "The church seems to be doing a great job in so many areas, but Mom is having a bit of trouble with the music. Could you throw her a bone once in a while?"

Contemporary Music – Another Take

Christians argue constantly about what they like and dislike with regard to the lyrical, musical and theological content of worship songs. Let's be honest: contemporary music probably comes under fire because it doesn't meet the needs of those with seniority. Most church services target the 50-plus age bracket. The fact of the matter is that youth culture is simply not a priority. Obviously, it needs to be.

The suppression of contemporary music often boils down to a debate between hymns and choruses where the traditionalists argue that old is better. Younger musicians are told that their taste in music is bad and that the shallow experientialism of choruses is dwarfed by the theological depth of time-honoured hymnology.

Certainly many contemporary choruses lack depth – I'll be the first to admit that. Current worship music suffers from underdeveloped theologies, biblical texts ripped from their contexts, individualism, emotionalism and misdirected praise.

I could stop there and join the revolution against popular worship music. The problem is that if we rely on the traditionalist hymns for spiritual depth, we'll be in even worse shape. Our rich legacy of hymnology is rife with nature-mysticism, neo-Gnosticism, low Christology, pagan overtones, a sanitized crucifixion, a romanticized Advent, glorification of the church, contrived theology-butchering poetry, and a health-and-wealth gospel. One example? Luther's *A Mighty Fortress is Our God* irresponsibly leads congregations full of Christians into ascribing praise to the Devil. Check it out for yourself. Bad – glaringly bad.

The irony is that current songwriters with their frequent use of biblical texts are, by and large, creating meatier songs than the classics. And so they should. The Psalms repeatedly encourage musicians to take the lead in community praises of Yahweh, commonly calling for "new songs." Faith is not supposed to collect dust. The mandate to write new songs may reflect God's expecting a continual outpouring of our hearts in the form of song, not a canonization of hymns from the baroque to the 20th century. Traditional expressions testify to the faith of our fathers. But without the faith of our children, the Church will not have a pulse.

Craig Ginn is a worship leader, songwriter, performer, and recording artist with SSCAN Records; his music is distributed by Christian Marketing Canada. He is also the Director of Soul Survivor Canada.

It was with such questions in mind that, at the aforementioned conference in Louisville, I asked respected American Baptist executive and author Jeff Woods that question I mentioned earlier: "Do most churches know why they are using contemporary music?" His increasingly well-known response? "No. I think that most of them think of it as something of a magic potion."

Worship and Music in Touch With Who's There

If Canadian churches find themselves simply opting for "the potion of the month," their music and worship are probably going to be largely irrelevant to their marginal and inactive affiliates – not to mention their most active and loyal cores.

- The research tells us that we currently may have a situation where 25% of Canadians are attending services about once a week.
- However, approximately another 35% of their affiliates are showing up anywhere from a few times a month to once or twice a year, with any number arriving on any given Sunday.
- That means that the real "seekers, searchers, and drifters" are, in fact, mostly individuals who identify with the tradition of the church where they have surfaced.

This is a critically important finding. It means that churches that are serious about outreach and evangelism will realize that many of them have an extraordinary opportunity: some of their "lost sheep" are actually showing up some weekends – on their own!

The clear recognition of the presence of such people would change, and needs to change, the nature of the services in many churches. For example, music that is "aimed" at outsiders logically would not be unfamiliar, new music imported from the U.S.; it would be music that resonates with their religious memories. Two quick examples of what *shouldn't* happen:

- A few years ago, a Catholic friend of mine attended a Protestant service with me just before Christmas. The minister of the church, in the name of not selling out to culture, passed on anything resembling a Christmas carol, opting instead for what might be called "Christocentric" hymns. On the way out of the church, my friend naively asked, "Why didn't they sing any Christmas songs?" A good question. Here, the Sunday before Christmas, on a day when there was good reason to believe there were a good number of marginal and inactive affiliates in the building, some leader made the insightful decision to ignore their religious memories. I hope someone benefited.
- On another occasion I attended a service where I found myself enduring but not enjoying almost all the music in the service. As I

scanned the bulletin, I saw that a bone would be thrown my way at about the halfway point, when the choir would sing the old gospel song "Softly and Tenderly." Always liked it; still do. Eventually we reached that long-awaited point in the service, at which time the choir sang the song—but to a different melody! I'm sure it was aimed at someone. I just have never figured out who that person was.

The worship and music challenge is an extremely important one for churches that are serious about trying to minister to their affiliates. The worship service is and will continue to be one of the prime points of contact with such people. It therefore is essential that the service generally, and the music specifically, reflect clear awareness of their presence and be responsive to their needs, while at the same time serving the active church core.

High-Tech Worship

In his new book *High-Tech Worship?* Calvin College professor Quentin Schultze tells the story of a worship service in which the pastor was welcoming worshipers "in the name of" when the Microsoft Windows logo came up on the screen behind him. "Worse yet," he says, "the computer program then blasted the Windows boot-up sound over the house speakers. Instead of hearing the name of Jesus Christ, worshipers heard the Microsoft musical boot."

He uses the example to symbolize the fact that technology and God sometimes compete for attention in worship. The same technologies that can enhance worship can detract from it – and not always so obviously. "Technology," he says, "has become a critical part of many church worship settings in North America. Interestingly, the church is growing the fastest in places like Africa and Latin America, where technology is rarely if ever incorporated into worship. But in North America, particularly in the U.S., we are the most tech-optimistic people in the world. We see tech as the solution for problems in education, in politics, in medicine, and now in religion."

Churches, he says, need to figure out what their strengths are and then consider how technology might enhance those strengths. "Technology," Schultze maintains, "needs to be fitting to the experience of worshiping God, but also fitting to the tradition of the church, its denomination, and its local mission. There is no one-size-fits-all approach."

In the end, technology simply expands the ways in which we can worship, drawing on worship practices, old and new. In keeping with what's most useful, "We can use voice and microphone, press and projector, body and vestment, candle and spotlight."

"High Tech Worship," Calvin News, Calvin College, January 10, 2004.

5. Organizational Credibility

It would be irresponsible not to reflect on the impact that issues such as sexual abuse,[43] residential schools,[44] and controversies surrounding gay and lesbian roles and rights have and will have on the ability of churches to minister effectively to Canadians.

The extensive publicity given to sexual misconduct, particularly on the part of Catholic priests,[45] and the legacy of the churches' involvement in residential schools have not exactly been good for public relations. In addition, the various positions that religious groups have taken on sexual matters – notably same-sex marriages and blessings, along with gay ordination – typically have been divisive within churches and denominations.[46] They also have been greeted with mixed reviews by affiliates who are on the fringes of Canada's religious families.

Remarkable Resiliency

Perhaps surprisingly, these controversial issues do not seem to be barriers to greater involvement for large numbers of people. You may recall that when we asked people what it would take for them to be more involved in religious groups, the factors cited after ministry by about 30% were organizational in nature. However, contrary to what many of us might expect, very few people complained about churches coming up short with respect to issues such as child abuse, residential schools, gays and lesbians, and financial scandals. Those issues – as important as they are – do not seem to be keeping large numbers of people away from the churches. As we will see shortly, other organizational matters are greater barriers to involvement.

I am not in any way minimizing the importance of these issues and implying that people are responding with indifference to them. I don't think that's the case at all. In the case of abuse and residential school issues, I think it's pretty safe to assume that Canadians expect their religious leaders and groups to be characterized by integrity: people who try to live life and carry out ministry according to their values. That's a given. What I have found over the years is that Canadians exhibit considerable patience with their religious groups and leaders. In the face of abuse or scandal, for example, of course they are disgusted and disappointed.

But most seem to feel that, overall, individuals involved in church life are trying to be decent people. Relatively few of the disheartened leave and don't come back. Even when their confidence levels slip, they attend services and pursue rites of passage.[47] In their minds, the church is more than individuals, and God is more than the church. They are clearly more patient and more forgiving than the media.

For example, the publicity given to sexual scandals in the United States involving Catholic priests has been enormous. In February 2004, the U.S. Conference of Catholic Bishops acknowledged that 700 priests and deacons had been removed from ministry in Catholic dioceses since January 2002.[48] Yet the Bishops' Conference announced that more than 150,000 Americans joined the Church on Holy Saturday, April 10, 2004. According to their press release, adults entered the Church in every diocese of the country and in virtually every one of the nation's nearly 19,000 parishes. Bishop Edward Slattery of Tulsa, the Chairman of the Bishops' Committee on Evangelization, summed up the resilience of Catholics this way: "I worried that the cathedral would be next to empty due to all the scandal news this year, but I was delighted to find that the numbers [entering the Church] were higher than last year. It is great to know that God is in charge."[49]

Similarly, this side of the border, in July 2002 the media initially seemed to give as much play to scandal in the Catholic Church as it did to World Youth Day and the visit of the Pope. *Maclean's*, for example, gave cover story emphasis to both, and proceeded to devote four abuse-laced pages to World Youth Day and five pages to what it called "A Church in Denial."[50] Yet as the 11-day event evolved, and particularly when the Pope arrived, a noticeable positive shift in media coverage took place. The result was a pervasive sense that the event had been good for Catholics specifically and organized religion more generally – a result that was not without its media detractors.[51]

As for the sexual orientation issues – gays and lesbians being bishops or clergy, being married or being blessed – to date, active members and other affiliates are personally divided, just as leaders are divided. The evidence suggests that, at this point, at least, the positions groups are taking on these issues are not barriers to Canadians being more involved in the churches.

In the case of morality-related issues, I have no doubt that Canadians' patience with churches and their leaders has been influenced by what we experience elsewhere in society. The kinds of people and situations we encounter in the course of working in companies, government departments, and universities, and what we experience as consumers and citizens and even as sports fans, reminds us that a lack of decency, ethics, and compassion, for example, is hardly limited to religious groups.

Not Exactly a Credibility Builder

A recent non-event should leave a few heads shaking. Richard Roberts' Web site describes the prominent preacher as a "dynamic evangelist" driven by the "compassion of Jesus Christ for sick and hurting people." The miracle faith impresario was planning to be in Toronto to conduct a healing rally April 25. Then along came SARS.

"I received a long-distance phone call from a young man from Oklahoma," reports Toronto pastor Grant Gordon. "With the best pastoral tone he could muster, he said he was saddened to inform me that because of the SARS virus, Richard Roberts had cancelled his 'healing rally.'

"Which seems a little strange. After all, Roberts also claims that 'Jesus was born to step into a world of trouble and bring healing and deliverance. That is the call of God on my own life – to step into the heartaches and troubles of people everywhere, to pray and believe God, and to bring a word of hope and resurrection.' Fine words, but no show. The young man assured me that Richard was 'standing with you in prayer.' I appreciate that, but I guess Richard was unwilling to stand with me in Toronto."

Cancelling a Christian "miracle healing rally" because of the presence of disease does a disservice to the name of Jesus Christ. Two things are absolutely vital to the integrity of healing vocation: first, there must be faith; then, there must be healing. The faith healers among us have some wonderful precedents to live up to, and a mottled reputation to live down.

"But Seriously, Folks." Editorial in Christian Week, *May 13, 2003.*

Significant Expectations

Integrity is obviously expected. But the research shows that Canadians also see credible religious groups that are worthy of their time and money as being characterized by additional traits such as openness to change and diversity and, frankly, being more positive and uplifting. They also want the religious groups to have good leadership. Others want to see them as having character and not bowing to culture. ✓

A glance at their comments shows that everyone is not going to get what they want. That said, the more general call for organizational characteristics such as openness, equality, and positive change are reasonable and should be both heard and taken seriously.

A Quick Replay: Some Organizational Factors Cited

"…enjoyable services…more open to modern culture and issues facing people today…less abstract…treat all people as equal…allow priests to marry…interactive programs…dropping the formality, ceremony, and bringing it down to the human level…recognize that women are significant…less involvement in controversial social issues…make it interesting, try new things…a strong focus on spirituality, greater acceptance of and harmony with other religious groups, less politics and power struggles…"

Source: Derived from Bibby, Restless Gods, 2004:224.

Years ago I heard a well-known and wise counselling professor describe being at a reception where a friend paid him a compliment: "One of the things I like about you," he said, "is that you are flexible." The professor said he was about to say thanks and take a bow when the person added, "But what I want to know about you is when don't you bend any further?"

Religious groups that are perceived as credible and worthy of one's life will similarly know when to bend and when to draw lines. In many instances, both virtues will be hurdles.

This takes me back to where I began this chapter. As everyone knows, good ministry is not exactly easy. It's going to take a lot of thought and work in order to address spiritual needs, respond in significant ways to people who are finding life and relationships difficult, minister well to young people, and have worship services and music that can touch the lives of active and less active people alike. Groups also have to work hard to be credible in order for any of this to matter.

Yet these are central areas where effective responses need to take place if the renaissance is to be realized in Canada. This also takes us back to "the God factor." If God is calling people of faith to recognize what they are up against in contributing to religion's rejuvenation, I think it's safe to assume that this same God, at least in the immediate future, will be both patient and even a shade resourceful as groups try to move beyond their bumbling and find creative ways of overcoming these challenges to effective ministry.

After all, what's at stake is a religious renaissance.

5

Clarifying the Response

W e've been giving a lot of attention to the importance of clarity: clarity in understanding the new story about religion in Canada; clarity in the face of pervasive myths about dropouts, switchers, and Christianity being on the wane; clarity about some of the major implications of the research findings for ministry; and clarity and honesty concerning a number of ministry challenges that have to be addressed.

If you are like me, you probably are starting to get a little edgy, wanting to reflect on some of the tangible things that groups might do to respond to what we are finding.

We are just about there. But before we start trying to shake up Canada, let's make sure we are clear on what exactly needs to happen and who is going to do what.

What Needs to Be Done

The major goals that are involved can now be stated fairly easily and succinctly.

1. Groups must give high priority to ministering to their affiliates.

Let's keep things in perspective. The project I am envisioning is not one that takes the place of current ministries to people who are already involved. Of course churches must continue to carry out good ministry to the people they already have. We all know well what research confirms: worship, fellowship, Christian education, and ministry to youth are among the top priorities of almost all congregations. No one is calling for a congregational revolution whereby churches abandon their existing cores. The issue has been stated well by Jeff Woods:

> I strongly believe that today's churches need to reach people who know nothing of God or the church. But these efforts should never be viewed as isolated efforts. No one program of a church can be totally unlinked from all of the others. If a new program does not contain enough of the personality of the church, the current members will question the validity of the program, and the new members gained by the program will think they have been marketed a false bill of goods.[1]

It is essential that the highly active and committed affiliates and their families continue to be ministered to well. However, wherever possible, it also is essential that the goal of targeting affiliates becomes a high priority at local, regional, and national levels.

Some people have told me that it has been a slow and difficult process to get congregational or parish boards, for example, to "buy into" an affiliate-oriented ministry.

- I suspect that in some instances the problem, at least in part, has been due to people thinking that what is being called for is a dramatic alteration of current emphases. That does not have to be the case.
- In other instances, it seems people seem to think we are talking about radically new goals. On the contrary, *this is all about pursuing old goals in new ways.* We are talking about how churches might be more effective as they engage in long-standing forms of ministry: evangelism, outreach, and ministry to communities.

Consequently, giving high priority to making contact with one's affiliates should hardly be "a difficult sell," especially when the facts point to such an emphasis being both necessary and productive.

2. Groups have to locate their affiliates.

In order to minister to their affiliates, groups have to first find them. As most of you are well aware, the good news is that this first task can readily be accomplished.

What's novel here, of course, is that most groups typically are doing things the other way around. They are putting the onus on affiliates to find *them*. It's as if the New Testament stories about sheep and shepherds have been revised to the point that, these days, God has had a change of mind and now expects the sheep to find the shepherd.

Here, Roman Catholics need to be careful not to, in effect, "blow their lead." We've been noting throughout that Catholics have an initial advantage over Protestants in adopting affiliate thinking. The reason is that they already work from the assumption that if someone has been baptized a Catholic, the person remains a Catholic virtually forever. Individuals are not treated as gone and "available" to other groups merely because they seldom or even never go to church. There is no triumphant annual "purging of the deadwood on the parish list" for Roman Catholics. For example, if you go to the national Roman Catholic website (www.cccb.ca), you will see data on the number of Catholics. What number is shown? Not the number of active members or weekly attenders; that would be the Protestant thing to do. Rather, the figure posted is the census figure of some 12 million plus. That, everybody, is "thinking affiliate."

However, one prominent executive with the Canadian Conference of Catholic Bishops recently told me that the advantage of already "thinking affiliate" might frequently be lulling Catholics into complacency. They know they have the sheep somewhere in the big fenced field and therefore don't feel any urgency to go out and find them and feed them. That outlook has to change.

What's more, the Roman Catholic Church at its highest levels speaks of the urgency with which it has to change. In the Church's *General Directory for Catechesis* released by the Vatican in 1997, normal forms of evangelism were acknowledged as important. However, specific attention was also given to adults who are "in need of different types of Christian formation" – what was referred to as "an intermediate situation." The Church said that here "entire groups of the baptized have lost a living sense of the faith, or even no longer consider themselves members of the Church and live a life far removed from Christ and his Gospel. Such situations require 'a new evangelization.'"[2]

That's my way of saying that, when it comes to locating affiliates, Catholics have been given a directive, not an exemption.

3. Groups must be clear on what their affiliates require.

A common assumption is that if inactive affiliates only "come to church," all will be well. They will be responsive to what others find significant. They will become involved in the programs and activities that already exist. They will want to stay. It's analogous to assuming that, if only people will try the restaurant, they will like the food and come back for more.

Maybe, maybe not. The only way we can know for sure is to speak with them and learn what specific interests and needs are prevalent in the communities in which our churches are located. After all, we don't have to adopt sophisticated marketing models to recognize that what churches do has to be in touch with what affiliates need. In most instances, those conversations with affiliates will undoubtedly reveal that

- *some things* being done are *highly relevant* to their interests and needs
- *some things* being done are *not in touch* with their lives
- there are *additional areas* of need and interest that *call for a response*
- there are some *additional areas* of interest and need that are *beyond what a specific congregation can address.*

4. Groups have to go beyond talk and minister to their affiliates.

I recall a speaker a few years ago who reminded his audience, "Jesus didn't just tell people to go into all the world. He told them that when they got there, to say something." I've been emphasizing that the point of following identification leads to affiliates is not just to locate them for the sake of uncovering them, or conversing with them just for the sake of having pleasant conversations. The purpose of it all is to minister in response to what is being learned. Again, I remind readers that I'm merely reiterating the steps used by Jesus.

Initially that ministry may consist of little more than conveying interest in a person who has been located, and communicating the presence of a congregation that cares about him or her. But it means *doing* something. In the longer run, it means staying in contact and working hard to be as responsive as possible to what a congregation is learning about the interests and needs of the affiliates they are finding.

Ministry is what it's all about.

Why It Needs to Be Done

There are at least three reasons why ministry to affiliates is so important.

- The *first* is that it is the most effective way that churches can reach out to people who are not highly involved. Identification signifies potential affinity; as a result, groups have a built-in communication link to such people. At some point in your life, a Jehovah's Witness or Mormon has rung your doorbell. How many of you have *ever* opened your door to find that the person ringing the bell was a Catholic priest...or a United Church minister...or a Lutheran pastor...or a Presbyterian minister...or a Baptist pastor? You may be among those I've encountered in audiences and classes who will say, "Come on, now, we're not into knocking on doors. We use other strategies that are more effective." All right, beyond relying on friends to connect with friends, what are they? My research, for what it's worth, has uncovered few. Following identification lines provides a concrete means of making the necessary connections to Canadians who are "on the periphery" of churches.

- The *second* reason why ministry to affiliates is so important is that if groups don't reach their own affiliates, the task is left to other groups who simply don't have their affiliation/affinity advantage. As we have seen, the research to date suggests that when groups attempt to interact with other people's affiliates, they have limited success because they aren't given a chance. Put bluntly, if *you* don't reach your own people, who will? Consequently, this is no time for abdication and buck-passing.

- The *third* reason for the importance of ministry to affiliates is that a large number of those people identifying with Canada's groups indicate that they (a) are in need of ministry and (b) are receptive to effective ministry. What more does God have to tell Christian leaders in order to get them to respond to such a blatant opportunity and responsibility?

In the Roman Catholic instance, I return to the Vatican's thinking as expressed in the *General Directory for Catechesis*, which is so explicit in its call to respond to Catholics whom I have been describing as less than active affiliates:

> A prime category requiring examination is that of the many people who have been baptized but lead lives entirely divorced from Christianity. This in fact constitutes a mass of non-practising Christians even though in many hearts religious feeling has not been completely lost. Re-awakening these to the faith is a real challenge for the Church. [Such situations] call urgently on the sower to develop a new evangelization.[3]

An important asterisk. If a given congregation finds itself in a position or place where it can directly address need with no access line required, of course it throws the idea of affiliation and related affinity lines to the wind. Let's not be ridiculous. The key is ministry. If ministry can take place to willing recipients – the homeless, those dying of AIDS, people who need advocates because of their powerlessness, and so on – of course churches step in. They minister because they must and because they can.

An example is the ministry being carried out in Vancouver by First United Church, a "no strings," multi-faceted effort to touch the lives of the homeless, transients, drug addicts, alcoholics, prostitutes, the sick, and the mentally ill. Food, coffee, shelter, clothing, shoes, showers, bathrooms, haircuts, telephone calls, and medical help are only some of the services available. The limited staff deals with government bureaucracies in going to bat for people who need and are entitled to such things as wheelchairs, nutritional supplements, help in custody disputes, and welfare. The church has also been an advocate for missing women – and has held memorial services for many. No pressure is placed on people. In the words of First United's minister of congregation and mission, Rev. Brian Burke, "We don't make people sing for their supper." He leads worship on Sundays for about 20 people. "We preach the Gospel 24 hours a day," says Burke. "Occasionally we use words."[4]

Who Can Do It?

Can every congregation and every parish engage in a conscious ministry to marginal and inactive affiliates? The answer is a decisive "yes."

What If We Don't Have Many Affiliates?

One limitation some congregations in rural settings, in particular, might face is that they simply don't have a lot of affiliates to work with. They may not even have all that many people, period, where they are situated. Concerning the latter, obviously if the people aren't there, their ministry will be limited to those they already have. I served a small Baptist church in Indiana many years ago. We had a core of about 40 people, and there weren't many other Baptists for miles around. The pool-size problem is one that is faced by smaller Protestant denominations in general. There just aren't that many Canadians who see themselves as Nazarene or Evangelical Free or Brethren. It's a problem that Roman Catholics with their massive numbers only can empathize with in a limited number of geographical circumstances.

What I was slow to realize back then in those memorable Indiana days was that the situation called for Plan B. Had I understood religious identification as a line of affinity, I would have known that, under the circumstances, the logical next move was to move on to other affiliates in our evangelical Protestant "family" who (a) were not highly involved in groups and (b) were not being pursued by them. Such a strategy still involves following religious identification affinity lines – just moving beyond one's immediate group to people in one's broader "religious family."

In Canada today, it means that a United Church congregation, in lieu of having many people in the community who see themselves as "United," would attempt to relate to other inactive affiliates or disaffiliates in the Mainline Protestant family: dormant Presbyterians, Anglicans, and Lutherans. In the same way, a much smaller group like Nazarenes would attempt to make contact with similar individuals who identify with Conservative Protestant denominations: "religious cousins" who see themselves as Pentecostal, Baptist, Alliance, Mennonite, and so on.

There is no shortage of affiliates. What groups have to figure out is this: With whom do they have the greatest affinity, lesser affinity, and the least affinity?

- For some groups, there will be lots of room to pivot. Presbyterians and Anglicans come to mind. Both can relate reasonably comfortably not only to Mainliners but also to Conservatives. Anglicans can also relate fairly well to Catholics.
- For other groups, the lines will be pretty strained pretty early. It's all a matter of thinking through where affinities and non-affinities lie.

A fast footnote: The manoeuvrability and image of some Protestant groups is seriously hampered by their lack of what amount to "good brand names." Three examples: the name "Southern Baptists" conveys both "Baptist" and American south, seriously limiting affinity lines. "Mennonite" sends an unsubtle ethnic group message. "Salvation Army" connotes warfare. In such instances – dare I say it – perhaps some name changes are in order. Failing such drastic measures, at least the existing denominational ties need to appear in fine print in church bulletins. But if that's necessary, it suggests the value of the names as "marketing tools" is essentially nil. It's something to think about.

Following Lines of Affinity: A United Church Example

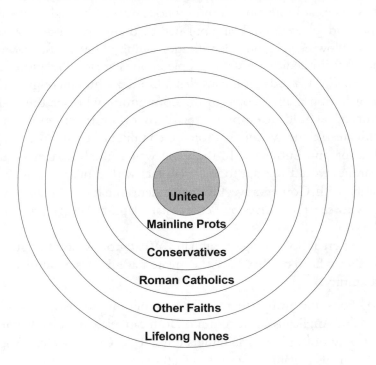

Reaching Beyond the Denomination – to the Religious Family

Congregations in smaller Protestant denominations typically add new people by recruiting along religious family lines – rather than only from within their denominations. Consequently, in recent years, there has been an increase in the tendency for urban evangelical churches, particularly non-Baptist, to delete denominational references from their names. They instead have been opting for such generic monikers as "New Life," "Northview," "Evangel," "The Meeting House," "Centre Street," "The Rock," "Victory," "College Drive," "New Hope," "The Meeting Place," "The Garden," and so on.

Officially, such churches would probably claim they are trying to be responsive to a society that is less and less denominational and even religious in nature. But, ironically, their primary appeal is to people who have a strong consciousness of "religious family," if not denomination – people who see themselves as evangelicals. What in fact these churches are doing is "marketing" who they are to Conservative Protestants generally, rather than only to people who see themselves, for example, as Pentecostal or Mennonite or Alliance or "non-denominational." In the process, Protestant denominations that make up less than 1% of the Canadian population gain dramatically improved access to the 8% of the population who identify with evangelical Christianity.

Such increased activity in the Conservative Protestant "marketplace" is undoubtedly adding to the overall vitality of the evangelical sector in Canada. Many of the churches in that sector are aggressive in their growth efforts and are drawing heavily on American expertise such as that offered by the Willow Creek Association. Retention of evangelicals may well be at an all-time high. There also is little doubt that "the robust market" is making for an unprecedented amount of movement between evangelical churches – an acceleration of what has come to be known as "the circulation of the saints."

What If Our Church Isn't Very Big?

Some observers, such as Franklin Pyles, the president of Christian and Missionary Alliance, maintain that one key to evangelicals having more influence in Canada lies with creating more large churches.[5] How large? Large in proportion to the cities and towns they serve. Pyles says that the four major metro areas of Montreal, Toronto, Calgary–Edmonton, and Vancouver can and should sustain many churches in the 5,000 to 10,000 weekend attendance range, with the three largest in the 25,000 to 30,000 range. He sees such churches as both resulting from evangelism and, in turn, functioning as "engines for evangelism" that transfer their expertise to other congregations, including new "church plants." He further sees large churches as playing a key role in ministering to the personal needs of Canadians – what Pyles calls "compassionate ministry":

> Churches with a large resource base must (and, I believe, will) become deeply involved in their communities. I believe these churches will offer a mix of immediate help, such as cars for single mothers, support groups, care for the elderly and very practical help to new Canadians, with an attempt at curing deep spiritual causes that present themselves in personal and social disorder. Using knowledge already gained by our compassionate ministries around the world, our large Canadian churches will have both the available expertise and the volunteer base to make a significant impact in alleviating a variety of ills.[6]

Similarly, the Centre Street Church in Calgary, a congregation of more than 4,000 people that is affiliated with the Evangelical Missionary Church of Canada, made some interesting points about the advantages of being large in launching a major building campaign in 2002. In speaking of why it was advantageous to get bigger via adding a new 2,000-plus-seat sanctuary and a children's centre, the committee organizing their "Giving God Room Campaign" offered the following rationale:

- A typical 200-member church has two full-time pastors and a full-time secretary. On average, its buildings and property – using Calgary real estate values – are valued at over $1 million. Ministering to 10,000 people would take 50 congregations – translating into 150 staff members and $50 million in land and facilities.
- Centre Street's enlarged campus makes it possible to minister to 10,000 people at an expansion cost of under $15 million, with a staff well under 150.
- In congregations of 200, senior ministers devote most of their time to leadership and sermon preparation; in a congregation of 10,000, most of the ministerial staff are freed up to focus on specialized ministries.

"Given the above," Centre Street's development committee concluded, "we believe the ideal church is a large church made up of small churches/groups."[7] Incidentally, one believer in such a vision was a cross-town Pentecostal church, First Assembly, which shocked more than a few people by donating $100,000 to the building fund of this church outside its own denomination.[8]

Interesting thoughts – and apparent generosity – particularly in view of the fact that we seem to have an awful lot of small churches in Canada.[9] Most are a fraction of the size of the kinds of churches Pyles and Centre Street have in mind. Maybe we shouldn't expect all that much of small churches.

A Bleak Reading of Average-Size Churches

Many average-size churches are losing ground to the mega-churches at the one extreme and the much smaller emerging churches at the other. The mega-churches are like Wal-Mart. They are doing very, very well. The emerging churches are like Mary Kay or Tupperware – doing well in homes. The [average size churches] are like mom-and-pop stores. They are in the middle and they are collapsing.

Tom Tan, church planter with Outreach Canada in Richmond, BC. Quoted in Christian Week, *December 16, 2003, by Frank Stirk.*

But let's not jump to premature conclusions. A closer look at the resource situation in Canada might lead us to conclude that maybe we should expect more rather than less from smaller churches. The assertion of small-church analyst Andrew Irvine is worth keeping in mind: "The small church is not simply a miniature version of a larger church. It is radically different. It can do things and offer value that the large church cannot."[10]

In one of the few published estimates of Canadian congregational size, Don Posterski and Irwin Barker claimed in the mid-1990s that "two-thirds of [Protestant] churches have 125 or less people in attendance on Sunday morning. And of these churches, over half have fewer than 75 people in attendance."[11]

Those figures were corroborated by Outreach Canada in 1998; differences between Conservative and Mainline Protestants were small, not only with respect to average attendance but also average budget.[12]

For the record, those Canadians numbers are virtually identical to U.S. figures for very small churches. However, Americans appear to have a lower proportion of churches with 75 to 125 active people, and a larger proportion of congregations with more than 125 core affiliates. In both countries, only about 1% of Protestant churches are so-called mega-churches with more than a thousand active people.[13]

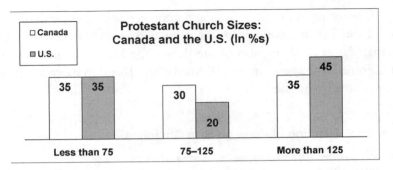

However, as confusing as this initially is going to sound, please stay with me while I explain: most Protestant *churches* are small, but most *people* are actually found in the larger congregations.

- In the U.S., churches of over 150 people may make up only one third of all churches. But they are the places where 70% of the people are located (see Table 5.1).
- Similarly, in Canada, less than one third of Protestant congregations have cores that number more than 150; nevertheless, they are home to almost 60% of all actively involved Protestants.
- The Protestant rule in the U.S.? Three in ten churches contain seven in ten people.
- The Protestant rule in Canada? Three in ten churches contain six in ten people.

TABLE 5.1. **Size of Churches Where People Attend**
"Approximately how many people are actively involved in your local religious group or parish?"

	PROTESTANTS	CATHOLICS	U.S. PROTS*
50 or less	12%	8	5
51–150	31	7	25
151–350	30	12	28
351–500	12	16	11
501–750	7	12	11
751–1000	3	9	7
Over 1000	5	36	13
Totals	100	100	100

Measure: average weekly attendance of church where they go.
Sources: Bibby, Project Canada 2000, and Bibby, PCPA Congregational Resource Study.

The size of Roman Catholic parishes is another story. Because Catholics are considerably more likely than Protestants to think in terms of "once a Catholic, always a Catholic," a given church technically exists to serve all the Catholics in the parish.

- So it is that just 15% of Roman Catholics say they are attending churches with 150 or fewer actively involved people.
- Another 30% or so indicate they are involved in parishes with active cores of between about 150 and 500 people; a further 20% are in parishes that number 500 to 1000.
- About 35% say their parishes have more than a thousand actively involved people.

At first that last figure sounds incredibly high. A naive Protestant observer would be shocked to think that about one in three actively involved Catholics attend "mega-churches," compared with a mere 5% of their Protestant counterparts.

However, what's really reflected in these figures is the fact that Protestants have far more "outlets" than Roman Catholics. Consequently, Catholics have fewer places to worship and participate. The result? Catholic churches on balance are larger than Protestant congregations. For example, initially I was rather amazed at how packed the three large Roman Catholic churches are in my home city of Lethbridge – even on long weekends, regardless of rain or shine or snow or wind. The turnouts are the envy of many of the smaller Protestant churches.

The reality that one can easily miss in all this, however, is that *three* Catholic churches – recently reduced from four – serve some 15,000 Catholics in the area, while about 50 Protestant churches compete for just over 30,000 Protestants. Divided evenly, the church-to-people ratios work out to 1:5,000 for Catholics and 1:600 for Protestants.

- If, on average, the three Catholic churches each had about 500 of their parishioners show up on a given Sunday, that would work out to a total of around 1,500 people.
- To match and even top that initially impressive total, the 50 Protestant churches only have to average about 30 attenders each, something they easily do.

In short, the Christian landscape in Canada consists primarily of lots of small Protestant churches (where a sprinkling of so-called mega-churches stand out) and lots of larger Roman Catholic parishes.

But that's only the beginning of the national religious resource story.

The National Resource Situation

When we draw on available records to examine the number of churches and ministers and priests that Christian groups have, and look at census figures for their number of affiliates, some fascinating patterns become apparent. Those patterns suggest why some groups may play a more active role in Canada's religious renaissance than others.

Here's what we find:

- *Roman Catholics* are relying on some 6,000 churches to minister to almost 13 million people: a church-to-person ratio of one to over 2,000.
- The United and Anglican denominations together have more congregations than Catholics: approximately 6,800. The church-to-person ratios for *Mainline Protestants* are in the neighbourhood of one church for every 700 people.
- Somewhat shocking is the finding that *Conservative Protestants* have more churches than *either* the Roman Catholics *or* Mainline Protestants. Well over 7,000 evangelical congregations have de-nominational links, and approximately another 2,000 are inde-pendents. As a result, the church-to-person ratio is typically considerably lower for evangelicals: about one church for every 200 people.

TABLE 5.2. **Number of Churches, Affiliates, and Ministers, and the Ratios: Select Groups**

Religious Group	Approx. No. Churches	No. of Affiliates	Ratio: Churches to Affiliates	Approx. No. Cong. Ministers	Ratio: Ministers to Affiliates
Roman Catholic	**6,000**	**12,900,000**	**1:2150**	**8,000**	**1:1600**
Mainline Protestants	**8,800**	**5,892,000**	**1:670**	**5,250**	**1:1100**
United Church	3,800	2,839,000	1:750	2,000	1:1400
Anglican	3,000	2,036,000	1:700	1,500	1:1300
Lutheran	1,000	607,000	1:700	750	1:800
Presbyterians	1,000	410,000	1:410	1,000	1:400
Conservative Protestants	**9,800**	**2,776,000**	**1:280**	**14,000**	**1:200**
Alliance	380	66,000	1:175	1,050	1:60
Baptists	2,000	729,000	1:360	2,000	1:360
Evangel Missionary	300	67,000	1:225	350	1:190
Free Methodist	130	14,000	1:110	140	1:100
Mennonite	550	191,000	1:345	850	1:225
Nazarene	170	14,000	1:80	130	1:100
Pentecostal	2,000	369,000	1:185	3,000	1:120
Reformed	270	116,000	1:430	260	1:450
Salvation Army	380	88,000	1:230	625	1:140
Wesleyan	80	12,000	1:150	85	1:140
Other	1,500	330,000	1:220	2,000	1:165
Non-denominational	2,000	780,000	1:390	3,000	1:260

Sources: Number of churches and congregational ministers estimated from data in the Yearbook of American and Canadian Churches, church yearbooks, and church websites. Affiliates: Statistics Canada, 2001 Census. All figures rounded.

What all these data add up to is a situation where *Roman Catholics* have a lot of large parishes. But the personnel – some 6,000 diocesan priests and 3,700 religious order priests, and about 2,300 members of religious orders ("Religious") – have extremely high "case loads." If, say, 8,000 priests were working in parishes, the ratio of priests to people works out to about one priest for every 1,600 Catholics. If all the Religious were working in parishes (which obviously they are not), the personnel to people ratio drops down to a mere 1:1250.

- Comparatively, the minister–affiliate ratios of *Mainline Protestant* groups is slightly lower, at one minister for every 1,100 people. The ratios range from 1:1,400 in the United Church to 1:400 among Presbyterians.
- The minister–affiliate ratios are considerably lower for *Conservative Protestant* denominations, where there is one minister for every 200 people. The range is noteworthy: highest at 1:360 for Baptists and strikingly low for the Christian and Missionary Alliance, where there is one minister for every 60 Alliance affiliates. *What is worth underlining here is the finding that evangelical groups report having more ministerial staff involved in ministry at the local church level than Mainline Protestants and Roman Catholics combined!* Many, of course, are part of multiple staffs carrying out specialized work relating to children, youth, music, small groups, and so on. Critics can bemoan ordination and staff standards all they want. But evangelicals clearly have staff in pastoral and specialized ministry positions to an extent unmatched by either Mainline Protestants or Roman Catholics.

I invite readers to corroborate the estimates I am making based on the best sources at my disposal, and remind everyone that the available data on non-denominational and "other" smaller evangelical groups are scarce. Since there are ranges of error involved, I purposely have rounded off figures to send the clear message that I am making estimates, not providing exact data. The exception, of course, is the affiliate information that is drawn from the 2001 census.

Still, the general picture is intriguing and, I think, potentially very illuminating as we ask the important question of who is able to engage in effective ministry to their affiliate pools.

Some Important Bottom Lines

Here are a few very quick thoughts by way of pulling all this together and pointedly addressing the question of "Who Can Do It?"

1. *Roman Catholics* and *Mainline Protestants*, in particular, are going to have to rely heavily on lay involvement if they are going to find the human resources to carry out effective ministry to marginal and inactive affiliates. Right now they appear to be badly underchurched and understaffed – one important key to understanding why their ministries to people on the edges of their groups have been so inadequate. As one Roman Catholic priest whose parish sits close to a provincial university recently told us, "I don't have time to focus on recruiting Catholic university students. It's all I can do to keep up with the people I have." This comment sounds irresponsible. Yet it reflects the fact that he genuinely is feeling overwhelmed.

2. *Conservative Protestants* are positioned to minister extremely well to people of all ages within "their family." In large part driven by intense commitment to evangelism, they are characterized by a high level of vitality and are frequently co-opting the exploding number of resources that are being made available. The resources include Willow Creek, Saddleback, the Alpha Program, Natural

Church Development, the Wagner Leadership Institute, Praise and Worship music, and a large number of regional conferences and rallies for both adults and young people.[14] Conservatives have gained more social and political clout through engaging in a growing number of joint ventures, as well as becoming increasingly involved in their primary umbrella organization, the Evangelical Fellowship of Canada. Such vitality and enhancing of ministries should only make them more successful in relating to Canadians who see themselves as evangelicals.

3. However, the growing strength of Conservative Protestants will not – as I have argued throughout this book – enable them to demolish religious family walls. Given their relative organizational strength, they would be wise to consider the possibility that God is writing a three-word message on those very same walls: "Share Your Resources." Work alongside like-minded Mainline Protestants and Catholics. Or else.

4. Is ministry to marginals and inactives something that only the larger churches can do? Hardly. Larger churches that have human and financial resources and are already committed to ministering beyond their walls obviously can and need to play a major role. However, as we have just seen, ironically, larger churches may not have the means to accomplish what smaller churches can do. Largeness requires a lot of maintenance. When you are smaller, you may have some time and energy left over to consider new possibilities. *Size in and of itself neither guarantees effective ministry nor precludes it.* The key to a full-fledged renaissance of religion in Canada would seem to lie in churches recognizing the importance of a division of labour that calls for the complementary efforts of religious families, as well as congregations of all sizes and configurations. ⎤

Who Will Do It?

You will notice that I have been around the religious block often enough to know that it is one thing to talk about capabilities; it is quite another thing to talk about actually taking something on. Sometimes as I leave an event, I sense that I was merely a speaker filling an annual program slot – and not much more. I started a chapter in an earlier book dealing with such feelings by making reference to this line about John the Baptist, no less: "Herod was greatly puzzled, yet he liked to listen to him."[15]

Are Healthy Churches the Answer?

In recent years, a number of observers have maintained that the key to churches ministering well lies with the churches themselves being healthy. For example, in his influential bestselling book *Purpose Driven Churches*, Rick Warren, the pastor of one of the largest Southern Baptist churches in the United States, has argued that if a church is healthy, growth will occur naturally. Health, according to Warren, is the result of balancing five biblically based purposes for churches: *worship, fellowship, discipleship, ministry*, and *evangelism*. Founded in 1980 in Lake Forest, California, near Los Angeles, Warren's Saddleback Church has an average of 18,000 people attending six weekend services. As with Willow Creek, the Saddleback message has been widely and aggressively marketed: the church's website reported that, as of 2004, almost 250,000 church leaders around the world have been trained in Saddleback's purpose-driven philosophy.[16]

This emphasis on healthy churches is also seen in the emergence in recent years of a program known as Natural Church Development (NCD). In the early 1990s, Christian Schwarz, a German studying church growth, explored the question of why some churches thrive and others do not. He carried out a major international survey project that involved more than a thousand churches in 32 countries on five continents. Schwarz claimed that every church of every tradition and culture, thriving or otherwise, had the same eight components: *leadership, ministry, spirituality, structures, worship, small groups, evangelism, and relationships*.

Healthy Churches: A Criteria Comparison

SADDLEBACK	NCD	RC CATECHESIS*
1. Worship	1. Worship	1. Liturgical life
2. Fellowship	2. Relationships	2. Community
3. Discipleship	3. Spirituality	3. Formation
4. Ministry	4. Ministry	4. Mission
5. Evangelism	5. Evangelism	5. Evangelization
	6. Leadership	
	7. Structures	
	8. Small groups	

Source: Individual #87; mission #105.

Thriving congregations, according to Schwarz, stood out as being characterized by higher quality in each area – having empowering leaders, gift-oriented ministry, passionate spirituality, functional structures, inspiring worship, holistic small groups, needs-based evangelism, and loving relationships. Schwarz maintains that there is a high correlation between the quality of those eight characteristics and a congregation's numerical growth. A congregation does not get better by getting bigger. But as it becomes healthier, it is likely to include and keep new people. A four-page survey developed by Schwarz permits congregations to measure the quality of the eight characteristics, with the results compared with a national standard. The task then becomes one of bringing a church to health in each of the eight areas.[17]

The Canadian director of NCD Canada, Jeff Berrie, says that since it began operations in 1998, the organization has collected data on about 1,600 churches. Significantly, about half, he says, belong to Mainline Protestant denominations. Berrie estimates that about 350 Canadian churches are now doing the survey once a year.[18]

Healthy for What?

It may well be that churches have to be healthy in order to look outward – much like a person has to be personally healthy, physically and emotionally, before he or she can turn outward and help others. Clearly, healthy churches have positive things to offer to the people with whom they come into contact.

However, I think that caution needs to be used in assuming that congregational health measured by five or eight or twelve criteria will inevitably result in focused ministry to outsiders. Programs like NCD, if they help to build healthy congregations, are to be commended and used.

But, on the surface, the frequent claims that healthy churches will become growing churches comes precariously close to another "magic potion." Jeff Berrie points out that the survey is grounded in Mark 4:28-29, where Jesus compares the kingdom of God to a partnership between a man, who scatters the seed, and God, who somehow causes it to grow to maturity. He adds, "We have a responsibility in growing the church, and so does God." What makes me nervous is when he adds, "Our responsibility is to make sure the church is healthy. God's responsibility is to then grow the church."[19]

Does church health all by itself produce growth in the form of outreach to people requiring ministry? Is it solely up to God? Or does God call healthy churches to go out and "grow the church"? I'm inclined to think the latter. In fact, I have no doubt about it.

If so, what is needed in Canada today is not merely healthy churches. That takes us back to the parable about drill bits and holes and to means–end inversion. So what if the churches are healthy and people still aren't receiving the ministry they require? The drill bits might be great but the companies will still be floundering.

What's needed so badly today is a commitment on the part of churches – which, perhaps like the rest of us, are experiencing varying degrees of health – to do what they can by way of moving beyond ministries that are turned inward, and reaching out to Canadians who need ministry. Preoccupation with church health *per se* can result in narcissistic mirror-gazing at a time when God seems to be calling churches to leave their dressing rooms and get on the stage.

In the end, I don't know who exactly is going to come through and seriously begin to embark on the things that need to be done. But obviously I have faith that some readers will, or I wouldn't have taken the time to put all this to paper. I'd like to think you are among them – or you wouldn't be taking the time to wade through it.

As I said earlier, my travels across the country over the past three decades have put me in touch with many gifted people. They work in a rich range of religious settings, many of which were unfamiliar to me when I started studying religion in Canada. I know well what most of you know: that there are men and women whose vision of ministry goes well beyond servicing family shrines and expanding the property holdings of insular religious clubs. They are not satisfied merely with building local empires or living with the illusion that "servicing saints" is the same thing as "saving sinners." I know that they, like me, are aware of the great need for the Church in our time to minister well to the committed core, yet respond to God's mandate to "go into all the world," beginning with the people living around them in rural areas, in neighbourhoods, in cities.

They are among those who must see what many will never see, and provide the necessary leadership to ensure that people on the fringes of Protestant and Catholic church life are rediscovered.

They also are looking at tangible ways for such ministry to take place – the focus of the remaining two chapters.

Bibby's Top Ten List of Excuses from Those Who Won't Respond

10. "Did you say someone did a survey on religion in Canada?"

9. "If we are growing, what's the problem?"

8. "That's interesting stuff. Our church, though, is different."

7. "I'd like to help. But we are renovating the sanctuary; the parking lot is next. Excuse me — can't be late for the church banquet."

6. "Those affiliates you speak of are a bitter bunch. I'd rather start from scratch."

5. "Frankly, I'm not sure what we'd do with all those new people. I kind of like things the way they are."

4. "Thanks, but I'm looking for an easier solution — preferably a magical...I mean, spiritual one."

3. "We just took him off our list. Now you want us to talk to him?"

2. "We prefer to take our cues from the Americans."

1. "Sorry, but I dozed off reading your tables. What were you trying to say?"

Getting on with It! Where to Start

L et's be honest. Religious conferences are often a lot like pep rallies: a time to give everyone a temporary morale boost. Speakers are booked, people fly in, sessions are full, people are polite, emotions run high, everyone's appreciative – some even excited. A few buy the speaker's books. But, in the end, I'm not sure that all that much really happens. I suspect that when people get home, life continues on pretty much as usual, including marking the calendar for the same conference, in Neil Simon's parlance, "same time next year." And like the morning after the party, a few people wonder how they ended up with a book.

Hey, don't get defensive. Academic conferences are not a whole lot different. We typically gather somewhere nice to present papers, in-form our insular mini-worlds what we have been finding, sit in on an array of presentation sessions (all right, maybe two...okay, at least one) where we reciprocate by listening to colleagues, miss the last morning's sessions in order to make our flights (or because we are just too doggone tired), and head home. Oh, here's a shocker: the most enjoyable part of those annual meetings is visiting with friends: in hallways, during site tours, over lunches and dinners and drinks. The day after, when we are all back home, the world goes on the same as it did before.

Beyond pep rallies and academic musings, significant organiza-tional change is something that is deliberate. It involves coming up with explicit plans and then figuring out how those plans can be "operationalized" – put into motion. Robert Bellah of Berkeley probably put his finger on one reason that academics – especially social scientists –

have so little impact on social change when he observed a number of years ago, "Academics spend most of their careers talking to each other."[1] They don't even get the word out, let alone work through policy implications and strategies for implementation. Thank goodness we talk to our students, or not much of what we are up to would ever "get out there," let alone have a mathematical chance of being acted upon.

And thank goodness I have the chance to speak with people like you. Since the mid-'70s I've had the opportunity to emerge from the barren coulees of southern Alberta and discuss my research findings and book material with people across the country. By now that's worked out to a large number of conversations with lots of highly competent and deeply committed people in a wide array of Christian settings. From the outset, they've been particularly helpful because (a) they aren't gullible, (b) they have a vested interest in making sure I've got things right, and (c) they want to know what the findings mean for ministry.

Few people in my audiences have been interested for very long in data as such. I've found that the research findings have held their interest for about 45 minutes or until the coffee break, whichever comes first. I sometimes have thought that the writer of the book of Acts was secretly taking notes at some of my presentation breaks when he wrote, "Perplexed," they asked one another, "'What does this mean?'"[2] After they have had their coffee, done some conferring, and looked at their watches, they frequently arrive back surprisingly surly. By that second session, most have wanted to know what I think the implications are for life and ministry, and what – if anything – they should consider doing differently.

As a result, this chapter is anything but a one-man show. Rather than being the bare-bones thoughts of one congregationally challenged sociologist, the material is something of a synthesis of the thinking that has been going on for some time between leaders and myself. Over the years I have "pushed" audiences and they have "pushed" me, as we have struggled together to figure out what needs to be done. Gradually, a step-by-step methodology has evolved to the point where it now seems to resonate well with "people out there on the lines" as something that both is doable and "works."

If you are a conference junkie who prefers good feelings and rallying cries to action, this is probably not for you. If you enjoy the occasional good conference but also want to make sure that Canadians who need good ministry receive it, then we're on the same wavelength.

The Core Components

There seem to be five key parts to what we might call "The Reconnection Method":

1. a search
2. a conversation
3. an assessment of needs
4. an evaluation of resources
5. ministry.

- The *first* step is to locate affiliates – more specifically, marginal affiliates, inactive affiliates, and disaffiliates who are not highly involved in their identification groups.
- Once such people have been located, there is no substitute for the *second* step, and that's to have a face-to-face conversation with them in order to explore their interests and needs. Sometimes it occurs naturally in the early stages; other times it has to be arranged.
- The *third* component – an assessment of needs – is necessary to process the results of the conversations. Organizationally, a resource group is required that can reflect on the kinds of needs and interests that are being uncovered.
- An evaluation of resources is the *fourth* element of the methodology. The resource group, the leadership, and the congregation as a whole need to evaluate the extent to which the church is capable of responding to what is being found.
- *Fifth*, groups need to minister as they are able: now, soon, and later.

1. Finding the Affiliates

This is the first tangible step that needs to be taken. It's so obvious, but it's a step that many churches never take. It's like my little girl at 18 months not wanting to let go of the chair and take a step or two on her own. It's akin to the singer who hears the music start to play but suddenly is immobilized by a serious case of stage fright. It's like bouncing up and down on the diving board but not wanting to actually jump into the water. It's similar to the author who is giving you a string of illustrations and not getting on with the book. You get the picture.

There is no need to pretend there is a mystery to finding affiliates. Three primary methods can be used: (1) a religious census, (2) cataloguing through contact, and (3) brainstorming.[3]

The Lost Sheep Approach: Carrying out a Census

The first method, which some of you have used, involves canvassing an area in order to determine the religious identification of residents. To lighten the workload and add credibility to the project, this is ideally a collaborative effort involving a number of groups. Individuals literally go from door to door, and have a very short conversation in which they probe religious identification. Canvassing follows in the time-honoured tradition of shepherds pursuing sheep.

I never thought I would say it, but it's about time I did: this method can be tough and is not necessarily all that effective. Most of you know why.

- People in larger cities, for example, often live in high-rise buildings and, as such, are not accessible. Canvassers typically either cannot get in the front doors or are told to stay out.
- A stranger who rings our doorbell is not exactly greeted with enthusiasm. If we don't know the person, we invariably assume he or she is (a) selling a product, (b) trying to raise money, (c) a Mormon or Jehovah's Witness, or (d) dangerous. Our 2000 national survey found that about 25% of Canadian adults feel that "a person who shows you attention is probably up to something" – a sentiment with which 40% of teenagers concur. Consequently, these days it's not exactly exciting and uplifting to be a door knocker. What's more, to do so is to invite vulnerability. Sheep weren't supposed to be mean-spirited or particularly aggressive.
- As a survey researcher I can also say with some authority that data collection of any kind has become all the more difficult because Canadians are increasingly conscious of freedom of information and privacy [FOIP] norms and laws. Sensitivity to confidentiality

and privacy is at an all-time high. To ring a doorbell and proceed to probe religious identification may be to invite not only resistance but also hostility.

If some situations make for productive neighbourhood surveys, great – use them. My point is that they may increasingly be a thing of the past. I suspect that such an assessment is good news for those of you who, like me, have always cringed at having to do door-to-door canvassing of any kind.

By the way, for those who say that a viable alternative to face-to-face canvassing is to use the phone and engage in religious telemarketing, I'd invite you to do a reality check. How do you respond to those invasive telephone calls asking you for money, telling you that you're one of select number of people who have just won a prize…or asking you to participate in "a short survey"? That's if, in an age of telephone ID callers, you even bother to pick up the phone. We all know the problem: "the reach" of such methods – the range of people they ever get to talk to – is incredibly limited. Pollsters, for example, who rely on the telephone to obtain those allegedly reliable surveys of "1,200 people, accurate within four points plus or minus, 19 times in 20," usually leave out an important piece of information: how many people they had to call. The telephone is not the answer.

Canvassing is sometimes extremely tough. But if it is, it may be a sure sign it's not the way to go. After all, you are simply trying to locate people; this is not a task that should be exacting anguish and pain and creating martyrs. If canvassing hurts, you probably should get off the street and find an easier and more effective way of getting the data. I smiled when I read that Canon Michael Patterson of Niagara, the newly appointed first director of evangelism in a Canadian Anglican diocese, hosted an information day in late 2003 entitled "Day on Evangelism for Frightened Anglicans." Patterson's point was that evangelism carried out Anglican-style shouldn't frighten people.[4] My point is that finding affiliates isn't evangelism, should not be intrusive, and definitely shouldn't fray the nerves of anyone. It's simply a search. It can be and should be an exercise that doesn't frighten anyone.

To paraphrase the Apostle of old, let me show you two more perfect ways.[5]

The Lost Coin Approach: Using the Information on Hand

This second method is, of course, also biblically based. It just doesn't receive as much play. Shepherds leaving behind the 99 to find the single lost sheep have always got the standing ovations and the press.

The prototype of this second method for finding affiliates is the parable of the lost coin, which, ironically, follows right after the parable of the lost sheep and therefore is hard to miss – yet is. Here Jesus tells the story of a woman who lost a valued silver coin. Rather than frantically retracing her steps in the neighbourhood or rushing off to see if she dropped it at the market, she stayed put, calmly turned up the lamp, pulled out her broom, swept the house, and eventually found the coin – right there at home.

Now here's a strange thing about these two parables: it's not at all clear that Canada's churches have been doing a particularly good job of taking either one of them very seriously. They haven't shown clear-cut signs of either going out after lost sheep or being on the lookout for people who have never left home.

If the sheep method has been scaring people off, the coin approach is almost fright-proof and potentially highly effective. It involves staying at home and being on the lookout for affiliates who are making contact with the church. Not a bad situation to be in. Here are some of the places we should be looking.

• Secondary Analyses

Some of you who had to put up with the monotony of a research methods course – the kind I have inflicted on students for several decades – know this concept. One doesn't gather new data but rather makes use of data that people have already collected for other purposes. In locating affiliates who are on the fringe of the church, a number of lists exist that might serve as a starting point for locating at least some of them.

One of the most obvious places to look is a membership list, a registry, or counterparts of some kind. In churches where formal membership is not strongly emphasized, the list might be as simple as a telephone directory or a mailing list. In some congregational instances, this could involve doing a bit of "archival research" if people who haven't been active for awhile have been "pared," resulting in their being relegated to non-active files. Researchers may have to retrieve older files or dig up hard-copy lists.

○ There are other secondary analysis possibilities – stimulated, perhaps, by keeping in mind that the reason we call the analysis "secondary" is that the list was put together for another purpose than what we have in mind. For example, I am amused (if at times dismayed) by the fact I seldom hear from a church that I happen to visit; maybe they assume I am just there in my research role. However, it's not for lack of information: each spring, churches have no difficulty sending me tax receipts. Donor lists might also include the names of many marginals, inactives and disaffiliates. Lists of children and teenagers involved in various church activities might also provide some affiliate leads. The point here is that this information is already available. It just has to be used.

• The Pews

As we saw earlier, some four in five Canadians say they are attending services at least once in a while.

- That total is composed of more than 20% who attend weekly (actives), some 10% who show up monthly (marginals), and another 50% who attend maybe a few times a year through once a year (inactives).
- In real-life terms, this means that, on any given weekend in Canada, an active core is joined by a sizable number of marginal and inactive affiliates.

- How many? Well, surveys tell us that about 35% of Canadians have attended a service in approximately the past seven days.[6] Given that as many as 25% attend every week, this means that 10% are *not* weekly attenders.

- This translates into a situation where perhaps as many as 25% of the people who are present at a service on any given Sunday are *not* weekly attenders. That's the national average; obviously there are congregational variations.

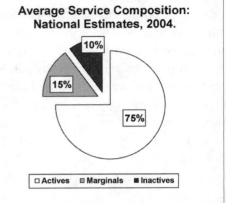

Average Service Composition: National Estimates, 2004.

10%
15%
75%

□ Actives □ Marginals ■ Inactives

- During times such as Christmas and Easter, that 25% figure rises, particularly in the case of Roman Catholics and Mainline Protestants.

What these findings mean is that there are a lot of marginal and inactive affiliates in churches on Sunday – every week. The good news for outreach-minded congregations is that they do not have to be found via sneaking into high-rises or struggling to get a two-minute hearing at a front door. The people they are looking for are in the building.

Mind you, they have to be "tagged." Cataloguing people who are requesting weddings, baptisms, and funerals is easy. Where more creativity – not to mention social skills – is needed is in finding ways of getting basic information out of the occasional attenders. There is no need to be obnoxious, but it's essential to find out who they are.

- Standard mechanisms, of course, include visitor cards, a guest book, and a polite conversation as the person leaves the church.

- Also common are interpersonal greetings during the service or after the service; however, the information gained is typically limited to a first name at most.

- The greeting of visitors during announcements is fine, but requires more. By the way, asking them to raise their hands or stand up – or, as one Atlanta church made yours truly do on one occasion, wear a badge complete with a ribbon and flower – is going too far in the wrong direction.

- Post-service social times are attractive to new active affiliates, but usually have limited appeal to less involved affiliates who often want to just quietly slip out the door.
- Designated "greeters" are potentially offensive, in that they may well be seen as information specialists who are to be avoided at all costs – especially if they make the mistake of trying to extract biographical information as people enter the church. They also are not necessarily the individuals with whom the affiliate "visitor" cares to get particularly personal.

As you know well, there is no magical answer. In a perfect world, someone in the church would recognize the individual and, after extending a greeting, introduce him or her to the minister or priest. In lieu of a solution like that, it seems to me that the onus lies on the minister or a ministry staff member to welcome an individual, and provide an introduction that enables them to learn the affiliate's name – supplementing the introduction, where possible, by inviting the individual to sign the church guest book.

But however it's done, it needs to be done.

• Rites Requests

We also noted earlier that the demand for rites of passage relating to marriage, birth and death readily exceeds the level of active weekly attendance. There has been a lot of talk about people who marry, for example, increasingly opting for civil versus religious ceremonies. The Project Canada surveys have found little support for such an assumption. In fact, overall, the demand for rites of passage has – if anything – increased among adults since the mid-1980s, and has remained about the same for teenagers.

What many people don't realize is that, sure, lots of people are opting for civil marriage ceremonies. But here, second and third marriages are getting thrown into the calculations. In my 2003 national survey examining what Canadians want from family life, conducted with the Vanier Institute of the Family, we found that 87% of first-time marriages have involved a religious ceremony, compared to 56% for second or additional marriages. The demand for religious ceremonies remains high when people marry – particularly the first time around.[7] I would remind everybody that those civil ceremonies also include people who, frankly, were denied religious weddings by clergy for any number of reasons. Otherwise both figures would have been higher. The success of "religious ceremonies without churches" – such as those offered by Rev. Allan Burnett at The Chapel at Stanley Park in Vancouver – in part seems to reflect the fact that such a niche market exists.[8]

TABLE 6.1. **Anticipated Rites of Passage by Group: Mid–1980s and 2000**

"In the future, do you anticipate having any of the following carried out for you by a minister, priest, rabbi, or some other religious figure?"

%Yes

	WEDDINGS		BIRTH-RELATED		FUNERALS	
	Mid '80s	2000	Mid '80s	2000	Mid '80s	2000
Teenagers	87%	89	76	70	87	86
Adults	19	24	14	20	44	57

Source: Derived from Bibby, Restless Gods, 2004:89.

Life's passages continue to be events for which the overwhelming majority of Canadians, young and old, seek religious ceremonies. When they do, their choices are not random: they usually look to the religious groups of their parents and grandparents. Contrary to what the cynics typically say, the ceremonies are usually more than "just for Mom." The ongoing activity of God in Canadian life – stirring up curiosity about meaning, arousing a sense of spiritual need, and leading people to believe and experience and pray, points to more. For many if not most people, the desire for passage rites is rooted in a sense that "God needs to be brought in on these events." Consequently, there is no reason to believe that the demand for such rites will diminish in the foreseeable future.[9]

If most Canadians are looking to religious groups for religious rites of passage of one kind or another, the implications for finding affiliates are staggering. Groups that simply are on the ball, vigilantly waiting for people to surface, will have no difficulty assembling an impressively long list of affiliates. Remember the woman and the lost coin.

Of course, if groups have not learned to "think affiliate and concentric," and also are not particularly committed to ministering to Canadians who need it, they will never see the coin. They will regard such requests for rites as irritating and define those who want them as exploitive religious consumers. In taking such a posture, they in effect will say, "There is no room in the inn," and send these marginals, inactives, and disaffiliates back out into the night to find their own mangers. Worst of all, many will sanctify such a "closed-door policy" by proudly announcing that they, after all, have standards.

I've been suggesting for years that, in the process, such people are mistaking a win for a loss, confusing being responsible with being irresponsible. If the affiliates cannot turn homeward, to whom can they turn?

The desire for rites of passage represents a major means by which Roman Catholics and Protestants can locate their affiliates. It's as if God is sending people who need ministry home – and watching to see what kind of reception they receive.

The Murmuring Approach: Brainstorming

Another important and complementary way to locate affiliates is for people in a church or parish to do some reflecting together about affiliates they know. One thinks of gospel accounts of people who, after hearing Jesus speak, "murmured" among themselves as a means of trying to clarify things. Groups that want to find affiliates need to do some creative murmuring.

- Maybe it's a planned session over coffee after a music practice, a Bible study, a board or council meeting, and the like.

- Perhaps another way is to sensitize individuals to the idea, and then have them spend a few days reflecting on people they know. In about a week, as requested, they forward an e-mail message listing, for example, five people who are either marginal affiliates, inactive affiliates, or disaffiliates.

Once again, you will notice that this brainstorming method does not ask anyone to bundle up with a notebook and umbrella in hand and hit the streets to get the task done. Instead, it involves recognizing that people already have a lot of that information stored away in their heads. Brainstorming asks them to download some of those mental files.

The closest, I think, that most groups come to using this method is by urging people to bring other people to church. The assumptions here are (1) that the uninvolved will want to come, (2) that group members will bring them, and (3) that once they have sampled the church, they will want to come back. All three are fairly precarious assumptions.

The method I am proposing is quite different. It recognizes that people often know the religious identification of their friends, neighbours, and colleagues. But it asks them to share that information with their congregations so that the affiliates can be contacted directly by the churches with which they have the greatest affinity – their identification groups.

For those of you who are into things like relational pathways to churches, don't get me wrong. The rule of thumb is still the age–old "Bring them." I agree with a recent Willow Creek Canada statement that people can be helped by caring local churches that are "connecting people in community" and creating hope and support.[10] But the new wrinkle is this: "If you can't bring them to your church, refer them to another." That way your group – and the group with which they feel greater affinity – can work together to supplement your efforts. In the process, the possibility that affiliates will be ministered to is greatly enhanced.

Another of my fast footnotes. I sometimes find that I make the mistake of assuming some things are self-evident when, I guess, they are not. In the case of the brainstorming method, maybe we should compare notes to ensure that some basic things about ethics are clear, including matters such as anonymity and confidentiality.

- When groups uncover their own affiliates through brainstorming, it would seem that they should be able to proceed to relate to them without violating ethical guidelines. Examples might include a Catholic who recalls that a new family with a Catholic background has moved in across the street, or a Baptist who notes that an Alliance "religious cousin" has just rented an apartment in their building.

- If someone wonders how a church "got my name," I assume a representative of the church would be honest and indicate that churches in the area are pooling some information their members have provided in order to minister more effectively to them and to the community.
- I also would assume that the people who provide names and affiliations of individuals would be guaranteed anonymity – that there would never be any attempts to link the information given with the names of the providers.
- Also basic to the process would be the confidentiality of the list itself. Only the individuals in a congregation who are directly involved in the effort to minister to affiliates would have access to such a list, and only for the ministry purpose. This is not a list for people in the church to use in the course of selling beauty products or life insurance. The information is strictly confidential.

These issues aside, I have little doubt that, even in fairly small churches, people would find themselves surprised to realize how much "data" they are carrying around in their heads about "the religious IDs" of neighbours and friends. Of course there will be significant variations, depending on where one lives. Still, such informal brainstorming would undoubtedly produce an impressive list of affiliates in almost any given neighbourhood, community, or city.

Toward Widening the Search

Individual congregations can do much to locate affiliates in their geographical areas. But a few congregations working together can do far more.

This takes us back to the issue of cooperative or "collective" ministry. If a number of churches in a given community or urban region would cooperate in carrying out such canvassing, cataloguing, and brainstorming efforts, it would be fascinating to see what could happen. The rationale is simple: when you go looking for your own family members, you find a lot of other people's relatives as well. It makes good sense to pass the latter information on to their families, rather than trying to bring all of them home to live with you. Such cooperation between churches would create something of a "feeder system," whereby one church's search for affiliates would result in other churches benefiting as well. Just imagine if two churches were doing the same thing – or four or eight, or sixteen. The locating of affiliates would snowball, resulting in nothing less than exponential increases in the number of affiliates known to any one congregation.

Realistically, this isn't going to happen overnight.

However, maybe it could start *within groups*. For example, United Church congregations in a given city, presbytery, or conference might agree to share information on affiliates, and put the administrative machinery in place to make it a reality. Similarly, Roman Catholic or Anglican parishes, as well as Baptist or Pentecostal congregations, might agree to local, regional, and even national coordinated efforts to exchange information on their respective affiliates.

Those would be great starts. But one would hope that in time the sharing of affiliate "data" would cross group boundaries, first expanding to the exchanging of information *between denominations*, and ultimately to the sharing of information *between religious families*. Such a scenario would see Catholics, for example, informing Anglicans and Baptists of people they know who identify with these two groups, and vice versa. Lutherans would advise Pentecostals of Pentecostals they have uncovered, while Pentecostals would reciprocate in passing on information about latent Lutherans.

I realize that such cooperative sharing of information about people already goes on informally to some extent. What I am talking about here is transforming that informal sharing into an explicit congregational and denominational policy, complete with the necessary mechanisms to make it happen. A local church example of the way things might work would be to take a page from the Mormon book and create a church position (such as "Affiliate Clerk") where someone is given the responsibility of keeping good information on affiliates who are being located, including passing that information on to other congregations when such people move to another location ("tracking affiliates"). To the extent that Catholics and Protestants buy into the idea and it widens beyond individual churches and parishes, it would mean putting the appropriate infrastructure in place to coordinate things regionally and nationally.

Finding Affiliates: The Collective Ideal

One church working alone
   can reach some people in some place.

One denomination working alone
   can reach some people in many places.

One religious family working alone
   can reach more people in more places.

Religious families working together
   can reach almost everyone.

The net result of such efforts would be a major increase in churches' awareness of the people who are in their affiliate pools. Moreover, as groups take the locating of affiliates seriously and share what they find with other congregations, "the Lord will be adding daily" — the size of the pools will be constantly increasing.

Such a situation, I think, would greatly enhance both morale and hope. Many a church leader, I suspect, would find it more than a little uplifting to regularly get e-mails informing him or her of the names of two or three additional affiliates who live in the community, sent by someone in another congregation — often from within their own denomination, sometimes from within their own religious family, occasionally from a person further removed.

Sure, it sounds like a pipe dream. But I think it's readily evident by now that, if the nation's churches are going to engage in a comprehensive effort to find and minister to the millions of Canadians who are on the edges of church life, it's a pipe dream that has to begin to come true.

Your church and group need to be part of it.

Connecting: Setting Things Up

A United Church in southern Ontario made a systematic attempt to implement some of these ideas. Their experience is both interesting and potentially helpful to other churches.

Early in the fall of 2002, a few of us at St. Marys United Church, a medium-sized congregation in London Conference, realized there was a large number of people on our Members and Adherents Rolls we hadn't seen in a long time. On a roll that contained 475 families, 98 of them had not been connected with the life of the congregation in any visible way in at least five years. We wondered, "How might we find out if these people still have, or still want, a continuing connection with this faith community?"

In November, 80 people gathered at a congregational meeting. Participants named 29 individuals who had "gifts for reconnection" – active listening, problem solving, a no-pressure approach, openness, understanding, honesty, wisdom, insight, patience, a non-judgmental attitude, a loving manner, an encouraging attitude, and others.

I contacted each of these individuals by letter and by telephone, explaining the congregation had seen in them the God-given gifts for such a ministry. I invited them to an evening meeting to talk about the possibility of being part of a short-term (six-month) "ministry of reconnection." Half of those invited [said] their participation in other congregational ministries kept them from participating in this one, while the other half felt able to take on the task. These 14 volunteers became known as "reconnecting ministers."

[In] our first meeting the group began to clarify its purpose and develop a draft plan to live it out. We emphasized the high level of confidentiality needed, since we would be discussing people's lives. By the end of the meeting we had come up with the following statement: "The purpose of this 'reconnecting ministry' is to reconnect with people who have been active members of our congregation in the past. We're doing this with the hope of

- helping them to know *their* congregation continues to think and to care about them
- discovering whether they have built membership connections with another congregation (in which case, we will transfer their memberships to those congregations)
- learning whether they would like a closer relationship with this congregation (in which case we will work to find out how our congregation can help to build that relationship)."

Each person was given a list of disconnected families and asked to take time to consider who was on that list and how we could best reconnect with them. The next three meetings were held monthly on Sunday mornings, before church. We opened with greetings, prayer, and a check-in. Then we moved into the task, closing with scripture and prayer.

Richard Bott, "A Ministry of Connection," Exchange, United Church of Canada, Fall 2003.

2. Exploring Their Interests and Needs

Thinking along the lines of sheep and coins and murmuring allows us to find people. The obvious question is "What do we do when we find them?"

I think it's fair to say that many people see the next step as inviting the located affiliates to come to church. Hmmm...but assuming they know where the church is, I gather that if most of them either don't show up very often or not at all, a simple invitation is not going to change things very much. If they wanted to be there, they would already be there. To recall our earlier imagery, our survey data indicate that most of them are not in the market for churches. But many are in the market for ministry.

Consequently, if our primary goal is ministry rather than pew filling, it seems to me that the next step is pretty clear: we have to determine their needs and interests. There's only one good way to do that, and that's to have a personal, face-to-face conversation with them – if we haven't already.

If this were a public lecture to a religiously mixed group of, say, 300 people, at this point a few of you in the audience might start to feel a bit on edge – especially if you are a Roman Catholic or a Mainline Protestant. You again might find yourself saying, "This is something that Mormons or Jehovah's Witnesses or Baptists do. Going out of our way to locate people isn't part of our ethos." Notice I purposely used a somewhat haughty word that helps to create some psychological distance and, in the process, neutralizes any personal indictment – sort of a verbal way of plugging one's ears when the message is getting close to home. Well, it's not going to work.

Those of you who are Roman Catholic, listen carefully. And everybody else, listen in. In the Vatican's 1997 *General Directory for Catechesis*, Catholics were told, "The evangelical attitudes which Jesus taught his disciples when he sent them on mission are precisely those which catechesis [teaching] must nourish: to seek out the lost sheep, proclaim and heal at the same time.[11]

A pretty straightforward message. It's time to talk to the sheep.

What Does the Conversation Look Like?

It may well be that a number of those conversations have already taken place. Consequently, what I'm proposing here is not something foreign to what most ministers and some laity are already doing.

- If the affiliates attend occasionally, presumably the congregation already has some familiarity with them. I assume that most of their names are already on lists somewhere – even as part of a "dead wood file," which one hopes was not mislaid or (moan) deleted.

- If the affiliates were located in the course of inquiring about a wedding or a funeral or a birth-related ceremony, a minister or priest presumably has learned a fair amount about them.

- If they were "uncovered" through brainstorming or from a source outside the church, the person who passed on the information probably already has some pertinent information regarding what is taking place in their lives. In cases where the affiliates are friends or neighbours, such information may be fairly extensive.

However, as necessary, churches need to make direct contact with affiliates and have an open-ended conversation with them. I'm envisioning that this would be an informal, short visit where the primary goal is to get an initial reading on interests and needs.

- Presumably the first few minutes will be a bit awkward, complete – in some instances – with affiliates letting the church visitor know they are not interested in "coming to church." That should come as no surprise, of course, if one arrived with the assumption that, if people wanted to be there, they'd already be there. In that context, affiliates might point out that they are ✓interested in spirituality, but not organized religion – a valuable bit of information for churches that aspire to bring something to the spirituality table.

- Like any good interviewer, the person from the church would focus on learning about the affiliate, asking fairly general questions about background and current interests – not unlike the pleasant conversation one occasionally has with a person on a plane or in a waiting room or some other place where we are socially captive. One would expect that, to varying degrees, individuals would touch on personal, relational, and spiritual issues. Perhaps the conversation would go from the general to the specific, or maybe not, depending on the individual involved. It may last 20 minutes, maybe 60, maybe a bit longer.

- Also like the good interviewer, "the church person" would be sensitive not only to what is being said but also to what can be observed. For example, the conversation may have gone in the direction where the affiliate is emphasizing that life is good and, unlike their parents or grandparents, they really don't need church involvement. Unexpectedly, an 18-year-old son appears out of nowhere and – unaware a guest is present – can be heard from the hallway yelling, "What do you mean I can't have the [censored] car tonight? I'm started to get more than a little [censored] off having to always beg… Oh, I see you have, uh, company. Hi." As he leaves the room, the affiliate tries to get things back to where he or she was – which isn't always easy to do. In the process, you hear a lowered voice mumble, "That son of mine is sometimes something else. Sorry about that." Maybe there proceeds to be a bit of mutual reflecting on the joys and lack thereof of being a parent. Unknown to both of you, the son is on the phone in his room lamenting to his girlfriend how tough it is to have to live at home. Life all around could be better. The experience, of course, provides invaluable insight into the life of the affiliate.

Who Is Going to Do It?

Who, by the way, should be doing such "intake interviews" when they are needed? Far be it for me to pontificate with a frivolous, easy answer from these barren coulees of southern Alberta. You know your situation. You know who knows who, and who might be able to speak with whom with the greatest ease.

- Sometimes the information is best gained through someone in the church or parish who knows the affiliate well. Please hear me clearly: I am not advocating some "narc"-like undercover work. What I'm saying is that, in the course of our relating to people on a normal day-to-day basis, we consciously and unconsciously gather a lot of data on folks. Why send a stranger into a setting that already is being naturally accessed by a friend?

- In other instances, it probably would be most effective – and impressive to the affiliate – if the minister or, where applicable, a ministry staff member makes the contact and sets up the visit.
- We already have found that a major limitation in some settings – particularly Roman Catholic parishes – is the heavy "caseload" of clergy. As mentioned earlier, in such instances it's obvious that laity are going to have to assume at least some of the responsibility for these conversations with affiliates. The positive news is that, to the extent that (a) laity are well prepared and (b) good matches are made between active laity and affiliates, along such lines as age, gender, race, ethnicity, interests, and background, there's every reason to believe these conversations can be positive, productive, and even enjoyable.

Following Lines of Affinity: American Catholic Research

After the scandals that have rocked the Church, and the cultural forces that have pulled many people away from it, many Catholics remain steadfastly attached to the Church. These people should be appreciated, and this appreciation should be expressed in every way possible.

The more pressing concern, of course, is how to reach and minister to the Catholics who still think of themselves as Catholic but have fewer connections with the Church. The best way is through people who share their age, marital status, and race or ethnicity but who remain committed to the Church. Young blacks who are active in the Church have a better chance than older whites do to interact freely with young African-Americans who are disconnected from the Church. Divorced Catholics who are still active in parish life have more natural lines of contact with divorced Catholics who have fallen away from the Church.

Attempts to evangelize Catholics who are low in commitment should follow these natural lines of social interaction. Attempts to reach out across racial, ethnic, age, and marital lines are not as productive.

William D'Antonio, James D. Davidson, Dean R. Hoge, and Katherine Meyer in American Catholics: Gender, Generation, and Commitment, *2001:148-149.*

How Is the Conversation Set Up?

You keep pushing me on tough specifics, don't you? Fair enough.

Contacting people who have contacted your church – by attending or inquiring about a rite of passage – obviously is not difficult. The introduction has already occurred; the bridge is already in place. In many instances, these people already have been visited. If the conversations haven't begun to take place, they readily can. If anything, some occasional attenders, for example, may wonder why they haven't heard from the church.

Initiating a conversation with individuals who have had no previous ties with the congregation – essentially cold calls – is a different story. Some well-thought-out procedures and good social skills are going to be critical here. The last thing you want to do is come across as a pesky marketer or as someone who is simply trying to get people to come to church. What is essential is to remember that *you are neither*, and you can readily say so.

Once more, procedures here are hardly written in the stars. Different people will have different views on how best to initiate the request for a conversation. For what it's worth, these are some of the thoughts offered over time by my congregational practitioners.

One possibility is simply to call the individual, explain the reasons for the call, and try to set up a meeting. Chances are the call will take many people aback. They weren't expecting it...it came out of nowhere...they don't know the caller... "They want me to do what? Why?" It all may be a bit overwhelming and end up achieving little.

Another more viable possibility, I think, is to begin by having the minister or priest send the individual a personal letter. The basic gist would be that the church is making contact with people who are Roman Catholic – or, in the case of Protestants, people who have had some ties with the denomination – in order to learn more about how the church might better serve not only its active members but also the community more generally. The letter would indicate that someone from the church will be calling in a week or two to see if it's possible to arrange to get together at a time and location that works best for both parties.

At the point of the follow-up phone call, presumably made by the person who will do "the interview," the request may well be greeted with curiosity that borders on suspicion and defensiveness. Their initial reactions to the letter – "What's this all about?" and/or "How did you get my name?" – are now verbalized. Honesty is not only the proverbial best policy; it is the only way to respond.

- It's important to come clean in repeating the message in the letter about the church aspiring not only to serve its active core but also minister to the community – that one way of doing that job better is to get the input of some of the people the group seems to have lost track of.
- As for their name, it became known to the minister/priest in the course of the church and other churches reflecting on people they know who have had some involvement with their religious tradition in the past.

The hurdle here, as we emphasized in our discussion of affiliates back in Chapter 3, is that affiliates are not all alike. Remember those identification lines we talked about – that some are *tenacious*, others *tenuous*, an unknown number *tattered*, and many *tangled*? I suspect that receptivity to having conversations will differ; what I am not sure about is exactly how they will differ.

- For example, it may well be that people whose links to churches are "tattered" will be reluctant to talk. The folk wisdom is that they want little to do with the group making contact. On the other hand, some of these people who harbour negative sentiments may appreciate the fact they are being contacted, value the chance to vent, maybe even be ready to turn a few pages.
- Similarly, some of the affiliates with "tangled" lines may be fairly apathetic about such a meeting; then again, they likewise may appreciate the contact and, if the time-slot is not long and in a place where they feel comfortable, they may think, "Why not?"

Who knows for sure what the outcomes of such initiatives will be until groups try? Some people will be willing to meet, other won't. In the case of the latter, the solution may have to lie in less direct, more natural friendship links with a person in the group, or with people in another group.

But informal or planned, now or later, the conversations have to take place. Churches have to know what people need. They also have to send the message that they care enough to ask.

A Ministry of Reconnection: What Happened

Over the next month, the reconnecting ministers contacted 66 families with whom they had a good personal connection [six additional families had children who could be invited to Sunday school by Sunday school personnel]. All of these contacts were first made by phone, asking people whether they would be willing to have a visit. Interestingly, all of the people preferred to have a telephone conversation rather than a face-to-face visit. During the course of the conversation, the volunteer explained the purpose of the call and that we *weren't* calling to ask for money!

None of the reconnecting ministers felt that people were upset by the contact made. In all cases, people were either willing to talk about their sense of disconnection or felt comfortable politely stating they were not interested in having the conversation. Out of 66 families reached, only 6 stated they did not want to have a connection with St. Marys United Church. Of these, two let us know they were connected with other churches in the community. At their request, we sent letters of transfer to their new congregations. Reconnecting ministers reported that the reason most often given for lack of connection was that people were too busy.

The next group of people contacted were those with whom no one in the group felt they had more than a passing acquaintance [26]. One volunteer drafted a letter of introduction, to be signed by me, that would go to all of the families in this group. The letter stated that a member of the congregation would be calling in the next week and explained the purpose of the call. The reconnecting ministers reported that 8 indicated they didn't want any further connection with the congregation. Again, it was reported that most people felt their church life had fallen to the busyness of the rest of their lives. The group was surprised that there were far fewer angry conversations than expected.

In the two months that followed, we did some follow-up with those who had been contacted. A brochure was mailed out to all of those who had been visited. Nearly half of the reconnecting ministers initiated telephone conversations with many of the people they had called initially.

At least 10 families [came] to worship. It was exciting to see how these people were welcomed and invited to join in some of the community activities.

This has been an excellent way to build and rebuild the community of Christ known as St. Marys United Church. We strongly recommend such a process to congregations.

Richard Bott is minister of personnel at St. Marys United Church, St. Marys, Ontario. The full article appeared in the United Church publication Exchange, Fall 2003.

Getting on with It!
Where to Finish

W e've found the affiliates and we've spoken with them. That's a good start. What is critical is where we go from here.

3. Assessing What Is Being Learned

The third component of The Reconnection Method is assessment – reflecting on what is being learned from the conversations. Taken together, the conversations add up to what amounts to an extensive survey of less-involved affiliates. Both the sample size and the amount of data will continue to expand as more and more affiliates are located and "interviewed." We won't lack for information.

The Resource Group and Its Role

What therefore is needed is a clearly defined organizational means of dealing with what is being learned – a resource group that reflects on the types of needs and interests being uncovered, and assesses the Church's ability to respond, now and in the future. The resource group would work closely with people involved in other facets of a church's ministry. It would be something like the research and development wing of a company, carrying out market research that in turn influences the product lines of the company. [1]

Presumably the resource group would take responsibility for overseeing

(a) the locating of affiliates

(b) conversations with them

(c) the compilation and interpretation of "interview" findings

(d) the presentation of the findings to appropriate church committees or boards.

For example, suppose the findings were pointing to widespread interest and needs relating to three areas: spirituality, conflict between parents and their teenagers, and seniors who are feeling isolated. Having identified these three areas from the conversations with affiliates, it would be the resource group's role to evaluate the extent to which the current ministries of the church (1) are addressing these three areas and (2) should be altered or expanded in order to address these areas. The next step would be for the research group to communicate its findings to the appropriate church bodies or individuals.

After examining current ministry resources, the resource group might indicate, for example, that existing programs can serve seniors well if they are focused more sharply on less active affiliates, that parents and teenagers can benefit considerably from existing counselling and activity programs, but that the church currently has nothing in place that would allow it to respond to the diverse understandings of spirituality. The board or council would have to decide what happens next.

The Key Is Carrying out the Resource Group Role

I realize that churches differ considerably in their organizational makeups and overall "polity." The broad steps and tasks I have just laid out obviously need to be modified accordingly. For example, it may well be that the role of the proposed resource group is already being played by an existing church board or committee – one dealing with outreach or evangelism or community ministry, for example. In that case, what I am calling for is simply an expansion of their mandate so that The Reconnection Method can be implemented. It may involve little more than appointing someone to coordinate the program. In other instances, particularly in small churches, it may well be that much of the responsibility for implementing the methodology falls primarily on a single individual – and one hopes not always the minister or priest.

What is important is not so much *who* plays the resource group role but that the role is played. Without it, a church will have affiliates and some kind of ministry, but the correlation between the two will be precarious. It's like a restaurant producing a menu without finding out what people in the community like to eat, or a business college offering courses that no one wants, or the DJ playing classical music at a high school party and wondering why no one's dancing.

Affiliates must have an impact on ministry, or ministry will not have an impact on affiliates. A key link to ensure that happens is the resource group.

The Dangers of Finding Out What Affiliates Need

The idea that needs and priorities for ministry might emerge out of conversations with our affiliates intrigues me. It causes both excitement and anxiety. In my experience and observation, it is much easier to call on persons and invite them to reconnect with our existing programs than it is to make ourselves vulnerable to the possibility that we will have to create new programs and priorities if we take their expressed needs seriously. Conversations that are truly open could lead anywhere. I believe this is why it is much easier to do a visitation program which says, "This is what we have to offer" or "We've been missing you, come back and join us," than it is to take the time to listen in depth to our affiliates. By doing so we run the risk of discovering that much of what we have to offer is redundant or irrelevant to the reality of their lives today.

Rev. Jim Bragan, a minister with extensive experience in both Canada and the United States, currently is an Intentional Interim Minister serving United, Presbyterian, and Baptist congregations in the Maritimes.

---

4. Evaluating What Can Be Done

The resource group and appropriate congregational boards and committees have the important task of evaluating the appropriate responses to what is being learned about interests and needs. That requires a clear understanding of what congregations are doing, what they can do, and what they should do.

It seems to me that effective responses to interest and need will include at least four features: the ability (1) to turn outward, (2) to retain but rethink existing ministries, (3) to be open to the possible need for new ministries, and (4) to cultivate resource alliances.

Turning Outward as Well as Inward

Earlier I emphasized that no one is calling for churches to cease to minister first and foremost to their committed cores. They represent the heart of congregations. They've found significance in church involvement, and are providing the human and financial resources to make ministries possible. Their wants and needs have to be looked after. It therefore is essential that churches carry out good ministries to the people they already have.

However, if Canadians who are not highly involved in religious groups are going to be touched by ministry, churches have to take their needs and interests seriously as well. In many congregational instances, that may require a shift in focus from "serving us" to "serving them," too. It also will require openness to modifying ministry as necessary.

The pervasiveness of the inclination for churches to think first of "ministry to us" and secondarily of "ministry to them" has been well documented.

For example, in the late 1990s, I had the privilege of conducting an extensive survey for some 30 American Protestant denominational publishers. They wanted a reading on the resource needs of churches. The survey involved over 2,200 congregations and more than 5,500 ministers and lay leaders. Together, the participating denominations are home to about 75% of all the people in the United States who are affiliated with Protestant congregations. That's my way of saying the sample tells us a great deal about American Protestant churches.

One of the questions put to the participants had to do with ministry priorities. People were given a list of 24 areas and asked to indicate whether they saw their own congregations as giving them "Very High," "Fairly High," or "Not Very High" priority.

The top 10 priorities overall featured things like good worship and music, Bible studies, and activities for youth. Only one that did not pertain to life within the walls of the churches – supporting world missions – cracked the top 10 priorities. Areas that represented more explicit types of ministry directed to people outside the church didn't fare particularly well. They included "serving the needy" (#12), "serving the needs of the community" (#15), "engaging in evangelism" (#18), and "working with other groups to improve the community" (#20). "Attempting to address social issues" came in dead last at #24. There wasn't a lot of difference in ministry priorities by church size – apart from very small churches seeing sheer survival as second only to having meaningful worship services.

TABLE 7.1. **Top 10 Ministry Priorities of American Protestant Churches by Church Size.**
Ranking of Areas That Are Being Given "Very High Priority"

	ALL	>350	151–350	51–150	50 and under
Meaningful worship services	1	1	1	1	1
Good music	2	2	2	3	6
Trying to keep the church going	3	10	6	4	2
Providing a sense of community	4	6	4	2	3
Christian education for youth	5	3	3	5	9
Bible study	6	8	10	6	4
Activities for young people	7	4	5	8	–
Christian education for adults	8	7	8	9	10
Supporting world missions	9	9	9	7	8
Having good physical facilities	10	5	7	10	–
Denominational traditions & beliefs	–	–	–	–	5
Serving the needy	–	–	–	–	7

Source: Derived from Bibby, PCPA Congregational Resource Study, 1998.

Is the Canadian situation, including that of Roman Catholic parishes, any different?

- A national survey I completed for the Christian and Missionary Alliance in 1999 found that "meaningful worship services" was also ranked number 1, with no "outside activity" except "financial support for overseas missions" making the top 10 ministry priorities. In the list of 29 areas, "ministering to the needs of the community" came in #22, "cooperative efforts with other churches in the community" #25, and "attempting to address social issues" last, at #29.[2]

- A similar national survey completed for the United Church in 1994 asking how involved local congregations should be in 20 various programs and activities found similar ranking tendencies, especially among laity.[3] Good sermons and a good Sunday School/Church School shared the #1 position, followed by a church for the family, and activities for young people. Responding to community needs came in #5, efforts to influence society #13, efforts to address global issues #19, and evangelism #20.
- And Roman Catholic ministry priorities? We're not sure. Comparable data haven't been collected. What we do know from our Project Canada 2000 survey is that approximately 30% of Catholics do not think the Church should be involved in social matters, some 20% feel it should focus only on spiritual issues, and another 7% think the church should not get involved in people's personal issues. At a minimum, such findings suggest that – similar to Protestant groups – not every Catholic is backing ministries that focus on personal needs, community needs, influencing society, or evangelism.

These findings serve as a reminder that many congregations and individuals are going to have to expand their views of ministry if affiliates on the edges of church life are ever going to be reached. Right now, churches seem to be top-heavy with ministries to their active cores, and light on ministries aimed at people outside their immediate boundaries – including their affiliates who are on "the outer rings" of those concentric circles.

However, that isn't to say churches are unwilling to look outward. On the contrary, as I've been emphasizing throughout the book, we all are well aware that large numbers of Protestant and Catholic leaders fully recognize the need for their churches to look outward and have a significant impact on Canadians who need ministry. These people and their churches also do not lack existing ministries which – with some adjustments – can serve less active affiliates extremely well.

Retaining – But Rethinking – Existing Ministries

Our national survey findings suggest that extensive conversations with marginal and inactive affiliates will reveal interests and needs that will require some ministry adjustments. But before starting work on the new blueprints, it's important to know what parts of the house require some renovating, and what parts do not. Besides, before contemplating tearing out any walls, it also is important to consider the possibility that the necessary alterations might best be made by adding on another room or two, and leaving the rest of the place pretty much intact.

• Publicizing Ministry

In most congregations, some and perhaps many good ministries already exist that can serve everybody pretty well – actives, marginals, and inactives alike. For example, some churches and parishes have in place excellent ministries to children, youth, and seniors. The problem doesn't lie with the ministries; the problem lies with the fact that they aren't known to large numbers of affiliates. Ironically, they are the very kinds of things that the less involved say would lead them to consider greater involvement. Such programs and activities do not need to be revised as much as they need to be publicized.

• Supplementing Ministry

As we saw in our reflections in Chapter 4 on worship and music, the danger in changing "what is" in order to attract newcomers is that styles and activities and programs that are meaningful for the durable core may be sacrificed. This can be a big price to pay, especially if quest-minded Boomers, Xers, and Nexers turn out be largely illusory.

If churches are going to pull Classic Coke from their shelves in favour of a new brand, they need to at least learn the lesson that Coca-Cola learned: to do so is to run the risk of losing old customers while failing to recruit comparable numbers of new ones. Better to expand the product line.

- Adding a contemporary worship service is probably preferable to eliminating the old one.
- Adding a group session on contemporary spirituality in a local food or coffee spot is probably a better way to go than eliminating existing variations of Bible study and prayer.
- Giving new emphasis to small groups and cell groups to deal with personal interests and personal problems should not be accompanied by the elimination of events — such as a public address by a family specialist — for those who prefer large to small.

The Many Faces of Canadian Anglicanism

For many in the Anglican tradition, "traditional" forms of worship bring peace, comfort and joy. Some spoke about the light through the stained glass windows of their home church. Even the texture of the wood in their home church pew, the familiar feel of the pages in their book of prayer, are part of how some feel grounded in their faith. Some are troubled by the thought that these symbols of faith made manifest might change, or even be lost.

For many Anglicans from outside the Canadian tradition, these common objects are not familiar. They come to the Church from other Anglican traditions, ones where the churches look and feel and sound different from mainstream churches in Canada. Some long for their home Anglican culture, the music, the familiar perfumes, the textures.

Some Anglicans who worship with church communities that are somehow "outside the mainstream" say that the rhythm of their own worship tradition just does not move at the same pace as does the Anglican tradition in Canada. Some say that the rhythm of worship in the mainstream Church can be troubling and, for some, even foreign to their sense of faith and worship.

These observations were offered by Sally Preiner of the Environics Research Group (2002:104) following a first-phase, qualitative look at the Anglican Church of Canada.

• Diversifying Ministry

As readers are well aware, the lack of resources may often make it difficult to go the supplemental route just described. In such situations, it seems churches frequently take the position that it's going to have to be one style of ministry or the other, one activity or the other. In popular parlance, the posture is an organizationally masochistic "win–lose" rather than "win–win."

Fortunately, in the case of worship and music, many groups have opted for peace over war by choosing to diversify a service. As we have seen, some 50% of Canadian churches are having so-called blended worship services, combining the contemporary with the traditional, the new with the old. That solution is not perfect, as some people in the pews will readily attest. As Posterski and his colleagues have noted, "A worship service that tries to incorporate too many diverse elements may blend like oil and water. In trying to please everyone, a church leader may end up pleasing no one."[4] However, it's a compromise that tries to take the reality of diverse congregations into account. Of particular importance, it provides services with a built-in capability of being flexible enough to be responsive to the religious memories and religious cultures of a wide range of affiliates.

The blended worship service would seem to be the prototype for many other forms of ministry that are attempting to respond to the interests and needs of affiliates. For example, one could envision that, over time, congregations might experience an influx of marginal and inactive people whose spiritual needs include the desire for things such as a better understanding of the Bible, how to pray, and how to better understand death. Many churches, of course, already have existing activities that deal with Bible study and prayer. Some also run study series that cover an array of topics; death and life after death could readily be included. What is needed is an adjustment to the way those topics are approached in view of the increasingly diversified nature of the participants.

Similarly, on the surface, the appearance of a growing number of marginal and inactive affiliates and their families could be accommodated in many congregations by existing Sunday Schools/Church Schools and children's and youth groups. But the diversity that such new people may bring by way of previous religious involvement — as well as social characteristics that could include marital status, education, and income – would have to be kept in mind to ensure a good fit. Flexibility and creativity would again seem to be essential.

In short, good existing ministries should not be abandoned or radically restructured. Rather, to varying degrees they need to be become better known and, as necessary, supplemented and diversified.

Being Open to the Need for New Ministries

The fit between ministry and need always should be as close as possible. As churches reflect on what they are learning from their affiliates, they are going to find that there is disparity between what they are doing and what affiliates require.

Should they simply try to respond to everything that people want? Of course not. The resource group, leaders, and congregation have to decide what they can bring with integrity – ministry that is consistent with their understanding of faith and faithfulness.

That said, ministry holes can be expected to be found. Our national surveys document what many of you would anticipate.

- Many people are feeling they should be getting more out of life. Can that really be pursued in a meaningful way at church?
- There is a widespread desire for ministry that will help children "turn out right." Does the church have something to contribute?
- Others are dealing with losses – of parents, of friends – and are feeling very sad and empty. Can the church do something?
- Many – no, probably most – are having trouble with relationships at some level: with partners, children, friends, colleagues. Can the church provide some help?
- A good number of people, especially as they get older, are feeling anxiety over aging parents who often either do not live close by or require attention they can't always provide – there are only so many hours in a day and days in a week. Is this something that churches "do"?
- Some seniors have difficulty with some basics we take for granted: shovelling their sidewalks and cutting their lawns, getting to a doctor's appointment or a grocery store. But otherwise, they are still fairly self-sufficient. Can churches help them find solutions?

- And then there are thousands and thousands of Canadians who are feeling the strain of personal problems that are all over the map: health, aging, finances, careers, school, self-esteem, children, depression, sexuality, alcohol, loneliness and more. Can the church be a significant resource?

As the resource groups and their churches more broadly reflect on these kinds of needs, they will conclude that some things can be addressed well right now. What is needed is to bring the affiliate and the ministry together. Other needs may be in areas that have been badly overlooked...like seeing if some of the younger people in the church might make themselves available to shovel a walk or cut a lawn...or having a layperson drop by the nearby nursing home to visit the father or mother of an affiliate who is provinces – or even countries – away.

In many instances, churches will find that the resources required for a good response are not necessarily extensive. More often, what is called for are responses that are focused, thoughtful, imaginative, and compassionate.

The Indispensable Place of Imagination

Without religious imagination, is it possible to see the providential hand of God in our lives? The resuscitation of the Christian imagination is long overdue. By Christian imagination, I mean that inherent...endowment which alone enables the believer to think the unthinkable, to conceive the inconceivable, and imagine what can only be "imagined."

Much of the Church's own remarkable community-building power [and] evangelizing efforts and success has always depended on her ability to summon and call forth the religious imagination of the faithful. And in those times when this ability was lacking or found wanting in the Church, some individual, with considerable personal charisma, has risen up to inspire the faithful. Mother Teresa of Calcutta readily comes to mind, as do Archbishop Oscar Romero, Martin Luther King Jr., Pope John Paul II and many other singular individuals.

Jesus himself was a person with an extraordinarily creative imagination; whoever would follow him, even two thousand years later, must be prepared to use their religious imaginations in order to remain faithful to him.

Excerpted from Lazarus! Come Out: Why Faith Needs Imagination *by Richard Cote, 2003:9, 28-29. He is an Oblate priest and Director of the Office of Theology for the Canadian Conference of Catholic Bishops.*

Cultivating Resource Alliances

As we all know, there will always be important needs, however, that will be beyond the response capabilities of a given congregation – at least in the foreseeable future. That will often be too late for the person requiring help.

In these latter instances, ministry nonetheless needs to take place. And usually it can. No one ever said a single church has to minister to people's varied needs all by itself. On the contrary, churches need to know when to accept their limitations and learn to point people in the directions they need to go in order to ensure that their needs are met. There is a lot of expertise in our society these days. Fortunately, a fair amount of it is either low cost or free.

In some instances, this may mean referring people to another church that has a superb ministry – for example, to children or seniors – that one's church doesn't have and the people need. In other cases, it may mean putting them in touch with existing community resources: the school that runs a great program for toddlers, the faith-oriented counselling service, the provincial agency that helps individuals and families cope with alcohol and drug problems, the federal agency that assists people who need to move into new careers. It may also mean working with business leaders.

Tim Schroeder, the senior pastor of the large and influential Trinity Baptist Church in Kelowna, recently commented that the single most significant factor that is limiting the influence of the Christian Church in Canada is the absence of partnerships and alliances.[5] That has to change.

There is much that any church can do, directly and indirectly. I suspect that the God who seems to be shaking up Canadians and churches is not impressed with people who use church size and church resources to claim an exemption from responding to needs. Virtually any church anywhere can share in effective ministry to affiliates.

5. Doing It

All that's left is to do it: to find the affiliates, have conversations with them, assess their interests and needs, evaluate what can be done, and get on with it. There are not too many mysteries involved, and consequently there are not too many good excuses for not acting.

In the fullness of time – well, at least in the early years of this new century – God has provided us with a fairly transparent picture of the religious situation in Canada. And with the help of many "Godly" people across the country, it's possible to move beyond mere description to analysis, and from analysis to prescription.

While The Reconnection Method I have been describing may look like a static five-point list on a book page, in reality it is anything but static. As information on affiliates and their needs begins to emerge, it becomes what we academics call "an interactive model," where all the parts are moving and affecting one another. With time and experience, the affiliate interest and need patterns become more discernible. In addition, we become more familiar with the existing range of our ministry responses.

As our efforts to minister more effectively to affiliates evolve, the initial responses to affiliates who are variously located by a canvasser or minister or neighbour can be offered almost immediately. No need for individuals who relate to affiliates to wait until the five steps run their course. Ministries are in place and new ones are evolving.

But it's critically important that churches continue to carry out the functions of all five steps in The Reconnection Method, to ensure that people are found, a personal contact is definitely made, their needs are understood, churches assess what they should do, and, in the end, tangible ministry takes place.

One final point: having found affiliates, churches need to keep the communication lines up – whether or not "the conversation" was possible…even when people move to another community. Until such time as affiliates destroy the lines, they need to know that churches in Canada these days don't give up on their family members.

A central feature of all this is that individuals who are on the periphery of church life know that churches – with no strings attached – have cared enough about them to find them and make sure they are okay. I suspect that, in more than a few instances, that gesture alone will impress and move people.

And who knows what God will do from there?

Realizing the Renaissance in Canada

R esearch and the interpretation of findings do not take place in some kind of a vacuum. Try though we might, those of us who pursue research for a living never transcend our own biographies – nor should we particularly want to do so. Those biographies clearly influence how we put things together. They also provide us with insights grounded in real life. As such, they can add considerable illumination to what we are trying to study.

In my own case, my growing passion concerning the need for churches to find their own has been influenced by the fact that I have seen many family members and friends disappear from the radar screens of churches over the years. In most instances, the churches have lacked either the organizational mechanisms or the sheer will to send out any search parties. They have assumed that those family members and friends have dropped out when they haven't. They have assumed that they are not receptive when they are. They have assumed that they are okay when they aren't.

In these early days of this new century, I sense that the God whose presence I have known all my life is doing some intriguing things in Canada, outside and inside the churches. In the midst of such developments, some religious groups are continuing to function like clubs that cater to their own. They have little to offer my family members and friends. Other churches feel they cannot do much more than carry out the basics: provide worship services and rites of passage. That's fair enough; in the tradition of New Testament models, they are doing what they can. Hope for my family members and friends lies elsewhere.

As I have emphasized throughout, I am convinced that the resources and the will exist for ministry to take place that touches people who are not actively involved in the nation's churches. There are gifted and committed women and men across the country who are capable of providing the necessary leadership. What's required, however, is a clear-cut strategy that is informed by sound research and sound congregational input.

This book has been written as an effort to disseminate such a strategy. It ends with a call for people like you who care to take up the challenge of implementing it. And you know what? Along the way, you will find my family members and friends – and lots of other people's family members and friends – and their lives will be better for it. In the course of such connecting and ministry, Canada's religious renaissance will become an ever-increasing reality.

I'm audacious enough to think that Someone will be pleased.

Endnotes

Preface

1   Berton, 1982:58.

2   Posterksi and Grenville, 2004a.

Chapter 1

1   *Time*, Canadian Edition, November 24, 2003, p. 75.

2   For a detailed discussion of the limitations of the thinking of Marx, Freud, and Durkheim, see Bibby, 2002:228-233.

3   Cox, 1995:xv-svi. Cited in Bibby, 2002:1-2. A serious rethinking of the times can be seen in an array of books that has been appearing since the mid-'90s, including Schaller, 1995; Carroll, 2002; and Oden, 2002.

4   Berger, 1999:10-11.

5   *Time*, Canadian Edition, November 24, 2003. Lead story: Susan Catto, "In Search of the Spiritual," pp. 72-80.

6   Catto, pp. 34, 37.

7   This survey, entitled *The Future Families Project*, was carried out for the Vanier Institute of the Family. It involved a highly representative sample of almost 2,100 Canadians, including some 900 people who had participated in one or more of our Project Canada national surveys.

8   For a stimulating article on how people in the United Church conceptualize God, see Sinclair, 2003a.

9   Sinclair, 2003b.

10   Harpur, 2004.

11   Bibby, 2002:102.

12   Ibid., p. 138.

13   Ibid., p. 58.

14   For an interesting case of vitality in Ottawa Anglican youth, see Davidson, 2003.

15   See, for example, Walker, 2003 (United Church). It's not that these denominations have no numerical problems. But they are not standing still. The Presbyterians, for example, have been engaged in serious self-study in light of declining membership and attendance since the 1960s in a effort to turn things around. But their examination has also documented Presbyterian churches characterized by considerable life and growth. The study report can be found at www.presbyterian.ca/evangelism/declinereport, 2004. Similarly, United Church leaders and congregations are constantly finding ways of revitalizing congregations: see, for example, Milne, 2004.

16   Preiner, 2002:105.

17   See, for example, the program offerings of Five Oaks, a United Church education and retreat centre in Paris, Ontario, that emphasize themes such as youth ministry (*Neos*), Common Life Community (CLC) groups, spirituality, and social justice. The 1998 Presbyterian Assembly identified six priorities as part of their *Flames* initiative to be carried from 1998 to 2005: a focus on ministry to children, teens, and youth; equipping the laity; active evangelism; justice; education of the laity and clergy; and spirituality

(www.presbyterian.ca/flames). The Anglican Church of Canada's 2005–2010 framework for ministry included an explicit call to add youth ministry, evangelism, and congregational development to its priorities (see Anglican Church of Canada, 2004).

[18] The establishment of new congregations in new areas is a priority for evangelicals and, to a lesser extent, Roman Catholics. However, "new church development" has been a lower priority since at least the 1960s for Mainline Protestant groups – to their detriment; phasing out congregations is also a hurdle (see, for example, Milne, 2002a and 2003b).

[19] See, for example, Perras, 2003; Gonzalez, 2003 and 2004.

[20] An example of the adoption of an innovative United Church Sunday School program is offered by Knechtel, 2001.

[21] *Canadian Attitudes on the Family*. Conducted by The Strategic Counsel for Focus on the Family Canada, 2002.

[22] *Time*, Canadian Edition, November 24, 2003, p. 78.

[23] Cited in Bibby, 2002:90.

[24] This section draws heavily on Bibby, 2002:66-72.

[25] Higgins and Letson, 2002:328.

[26] For a discussion of this thesis, see Stark and Finke, 2000:259-274.

[27] Greeley, 2004.

Chapter 2

[1] Berger, 1961.

[2] Higgins and Letson, 2002:4.

[3] Galloway, 2003.

[4] Bibby, 1987:51.

[5] The survey was actually a series of surveys carried out over a 17-week period for researchers at The Graduate Center of the City University of New York – novel and helpful because religious identification is not included in the U.S. census. An example of media interpretations is Grossman, *USA Today*, March 7, 2002.

[6] Lorrayne Anthony, 2003a.

[7] Greeley, 1972.

[8] Posterski and Barker, 1993.

[9] Berry, 2003.

[10] See Roof, 1999, and Emberley, 2002.

[11] Quoted in Galloway, 2003.

[12] Walker, 2003.

[13] For details, see Bibby, 2002:39-46.

[14] Doucette, 2004.

[15] Plug, 2001.

[16] See Kelley, 1972, and Stark and Finke, 2000.

[17] Anthony, 2003b.

[18] For implications for Catholicism, see, for example, Struch, 2004.

[19] Statistics Canada, *Religions in Canada*. Catalogue 96F0030XIE2001015, 2003:5.

[20] Catto, p. 74. For an example of an Alpha course in a Toronto pub and other novel venues, see Lowes, 2003. Drama, dinner theatres, and musical productions are also being used by some United Church congregations (see Milne, 2003a).

[21] See *Anglitrends*, 1986; *Unitrends*, 1994; and the *Alliance Future Summary Report*, 1999.

[22] Posterski and Grenville, 2004b:6.

Chapter 3

1 Quoted in Sinclair and White, 2003:174.

2 See, for example, Hall, 1989.

3 This surprise is echoed, for example, by denBok, 2003a.

4 Sinclair and White, 2003:13,15.

5 *Time*, Canadian Edition, November 24, 2003, p. 76.

6 Bob Harvey, *Ottawa Citizen*, May 14, 2003, p. A7, and e-mail correspondence, May 14.

7 *Time*, Canadian Edition, November 24, 2003, p. 76.

8 See, for example, Posterski and Barker, 1993.

9 For reflections on the vitality among Korean Christians, see Couto, 2000: 18–20; among Chinese Christians, Johnstone, 2002:4–5.

10 These are concepts and terms that I began developing in some detail in my 1995 book, *There's Got to Be More!*

11 Bibby, 1995:43.

12 See Bibby, 1985, 1994, 1999, 2003.

13 D'Antonio, Davidson, Hoge, and Meyer, 2001:50.

14 Cited in Bibby, 1993:277.

15 The Anglican effort is described in detail in Bibby, 1993:260–261.

16 Hall, 2000.

17 This section draws heavily from Bibby, 1995:151.

18 Milne, 2002b.

19 Glatz, 2004.

20 Posterski and Barker, 1993:53–54.

21 For an excellent article that shows that similar religious family patterns exist in the United States, see Hadaway and Marler, 1993.

22 Bibby, 2002:42–43.

23 De Santis, 2003.

24 Cited in Orr, 1936:39.

25 Brouillette, 2002.

26 Cited in *Flash Stories of Impact*, The Leadership Canada Willow Creek Canada, July, 2003:1. Westview's website is www.westviewbiblechurch.ca.

27 Brouillette, 2002.

28 Some evangelicals are cooperating with Catholics, while some Pentecostals and Catholics are exploring their commonalities. See, for example, Jantz, 1999a and 1999b.

29 Illustrating the lack of acceptance of Roman Catholicism felt by some evangelicals, writer Marg Buchanan (2003) began a recent *Christian Week* article this way: "With less than one per cent of the French population claiming evangelical Christian faith, Quebec ranks among the least evangelized areas of the western world."

30 See Bibby, 1994:28, and Bibby, 1995b:10.

31 Baum, 2002.

32 In early 2000, for example, Baptist, Lutheran, and Catholic congregations were among 20 churches that carried out a joint advertising campaign in Ottawa's east end, centred around a simple appeal: "Let's Go to Church" (Lowes, 2000).

33 The event was held in conjunction with the Evangelical Fellowship of Canada January 30–February 1 at the Delta Meadowvale Hotel. The former head of the Canadian Conference of Catholic Bishops, Archbishop Marcel Gervais, was the keynote speaker. Organizers said there were 105 registrants from 75 different Christian organizations. For details, see Paddey, 2003.

34 See, for example, Baum, 2002, for an overview of the Catholic Church's increasing encouragement of interfaith cooperation. Glen (2004) summarizes progress in dialogue between Catholics and Anglicans.

Chapter 4

1 Bibby, 2002:179.

2 *Time*, Canadian Edition, November 24, 2003, p. 77.

3 Bibby, 2002:181.

4 For a superb example of the diverse ways that Canadian artists and writers conceptualize spirituality, see Todd, 1996.

5 Source: Presbyterian Church in Canada website: www.presbyterian.ca/flames/spirituality, 2004.

6 Henry, 2001.

7 Cited in Paddey, 2004.

8 Chattaway, 2004.

9 *Catholic New Times* editorial, "Gibson's *The Passion* Shows Few Signs of Grace." March 21, 2004.

10 Bibby, 2002:201.

11 For a stimulating exposition of the range of spirituality conceptions among prominent Christians, see Harvey, 2000.

12 Bibby, 2002:201. Regina Coupar recently has made creative contributions to the exploration of spirituality through art (2002) and personal reflections on the Psalms (2004).

13 Higgins and Letson, 2002:329–330.

14 Ibid., 381.

15 For extensive illustrative data, see Bibby, 2001:234–242.

16 Gillis, 2004:30.

17 *General Directory for Catechesis*, 1997:87.

18 Ibid., 159.

19 Ibid., 257.

20 Yaworksi, 2004.

21 The Roman Catholic Church, for example, is extremely candid about the dilemma of needing youth, yet frequently failing to attract them, as representing both hope and challenge. See the *General Directory for Catechesis*, 1997:182.

22 The results of the surveys and discussions of their implications are found in three books: Bibby and Posterski, 1985; Bibby and Posterski, 1992; and Bibby, 2001.

23 This theme is developed in detail in Bibby and Posterski, 1985, chapters 1 and 10.

24 Overholt and Penner, 2002:24,186,144,126.

25 Interview in Gruending, 1996.

26 Schultz, 2004.

27 Posterski with Grainger and Stiller, 2002:1-9.

28 Burton in Egerton (ed.), 1995:151.

29 Grant, 1988:230.

30 Nol, 1992:459.

31 See, for example, Sinclair and White, 2003:175. For an interesting exposition and critique of Celtic faith and practice, see Bradley, 2000. Helmers (2002) offers an example of implementation of Celtic worship forms in a Toronto United Church.

32   By way of illustration, see Dold, 2000.

33   Recent worship experimentation and responses to it are found in Sinclair, 2002.

34   Davidson, 2003.

35   For details, see the Presbyterian Church in Canada worship site: www.presbyterian.ca/worship/music/praise, 2004.

36   See minutes of the 126th Assembly, 2000, at www.presbyterian.ca/youth.

37   "ELCIC + Renewing Worship." Introduction. Winnipeg: Evangelical Lutheran Church in Canada worship website: www.worship.ca, 2004.

38   Schaller, 1995:13. One exuberant view of new music as part of a "new awakening" is offered by Redman (2002).

39   The data source for Canada is Project Canada 2000; the U.S. source is Bibby, 1998.

40   See, for example, McKim, 1998; Stackhouse, 2003.

41   Burton in Egerton (ed.), 1995:146.

42   This gathering of invited congregational researchers and leaders was sponsored by the Louisville Institute and held in August of 2000 at the Louisville Presbyterian Seminary. For one view of what lies beyond so-called worship wars, see Byars, 2002.

43   An overview of the problem of sex abuse in the Catholic Church in Canada is found in Gatehouse (*Maclean's*, 2002); a comprehensive overview of the U.S. situation is provided by *Time* in its April 1, 2002, Canadian edition, issue entitled "Can the Catholic Church Save Itself?" A superb overview of the difficulties facing Catholic clergy more generally is found in Higgins and Letson, 2002, Chapter 4: "The Curse of Clericalism."

44   For an excellent summation of the residential schools legacy, see *Envision*, Spring 2000. Large numbers of articles dealing with residential schools and the churches can be found in both *The Anglican Journal* and *The United Church Observer*. The Anglican Church of Canada's website provides information on residential schools: generalsynod.anglican.ca/ministries/rs

45   For analyses of American media coverage of the Catholic sexual abuse, see Silk, 2002; Reardon, 2002; and Walsh, 2002 and 2003.

46   Informative articles on the blessing of gay relationships in the Anglican community, for example, include Larmondin, 2002a and 2002b; Larmondin and De Santis, 2002; Valpy, 2002; and Bird, 2003. A superb discussion of the church's role in providing marriage ceremonies and marriage blessings to people – both heterosexual and homosexual – is found in the 2003 issue of *Liturgy Canada*, volume ix, number 3. Some helpful articles on the United Church's take on same-sex marriages include Milne, 2003c; Duncan, 2003.

47   See for example, Bibby, 1993:76 and Bibby, 2002:186.

48   Some key United States Catholic Bishops press releases on the incidence of such abuse include those of January 6, 2004 ("First 'Charter' Implementation Report Issued by Catholics Bishop Conference") and February 27, 2004 ("700 Priests Removed Since January 2002").

49   Press release, "More than 150,000 People to Join Catholic Church Holy Saturday." U.S. Catholic Bishops, March 31, 2004. Between 2002 and 2003, Gallup found that Catholics' confidence in the church increased from 42% to 51% (Winseman, 2003); also see Gallup's *Tuesday Briefing*, January 6, 2004.

50   See *Maclean's*, July 22, 2002.

51   See, for example, the derogatory *Globe and Mail* article by Salutin, 2002.

Chapter 5

1   Woods, 1996:124.

2   *General Directory for Catechesis*, 1997:58c.

3   *General Directory for Catechesis*, 1997:25–26.

4   For an excellent article on First United Vancouver, see Wilson, 2003.

5   A superb discussion and summary of larger churches from an evangelical point of view is offered in the special Spring 2003 supplement of *Christian Week*, entitled "Large Churches."

6   Pyles, 2003:2.

7   Centre Street Church, Calgary, website posting, "Giving God Room Campaign," Campus Development Committee (Your Questions Answered), March 2003:1.

8   Callaway, March 2002:5.

9   For a superb exposition and critique of large evangelical churches such as Willow Creek in the U.S. and Northview in Canada, see the Fall 1999 issue of *Envision*, entitled "A Close-up Look at the Seeker Sensitive Church."

10   Irvine, 2001.

11   Posterski and Barker, 1993:126.

12   See *Envision*, Fall 2001. Interesting attendance breakdowns are provided for a number of Protestant groups, including United, Presbyterian, Baptist Union, Atlantic Baptist, Alliance, and Mennonite Brethren churches.

13   Bibby, 1998. A recent examination of congregational size and correlates is offered by Woolever and Bruce, 2002.

14   Major conferences are routinely being held. One example: more than 6,200 participants from Canada and the northwest U.S. attended *Break Forth Canada 2003* in Calgary, January 31–February 2. This annual event is billed by organizers as "the largest creative ministry conference held in Canada," with speakers who included Willow Creek's Bill Hybels, and Southern Baptist Henry Blackaby, along with Phil Callaway, Tommy Tenney, Brian Doerksen, Graham Kendrick, Lianna Klassen, and a wide spectrum of musicians, including the Chris Tomlin Band (Callaway, 2003).

15   Mark 6:20.

16   Warren, 1995. Current data on attendance is taken from the church's website: www.saddleback.com.

17   See Schwarz, 1996. An excellent summary, drawn on here, is found in denBok (2003b). This entire issue of *Good Idea!* is given to NCD, including the experiences of some churches and consultants with the program.

18   Stirk, 2004. For recent implementation efforts in the Niagara Anglican Diocese, for example, see De Santis, 2004.

19   Stirk, 2004.

Chapter 6

1. Bellah, et al., 1985.
2. Acts 2:12.
3. For an earlier version of these methods, see Bibby, 1995a:88–93.
4. De Santis, 2004.
5. 1 Corinthians 13:31.
6. This is approximately the figure Gallup was finding through about 2002, when it ceased to do its national surveys.
7. Bibby, 2004.
8. Snopek, 2003:11.
9. For a provocative discussion of what the Church's role might be in weddings, see Hill, 2003.
10. *Update*. The Leadership Centre Willow Creek Canada. October 2003.
11. *General Directory for Catechesis*, 1997:86a.

Chapter 7

1. I'm reminded fairly often that market language is a red flag to many people in the churches. That's unfortunate. I obviously think it can be helpful. Not that it will help much, but as the critics are well aware, Jesus himself used a lot of rural economic language, not only about shepherds and sheep, but also about farmers and wheatfields, planting and harvests. Consequently, if he were illustrating his ideas today, I think there's a very good chance that he would be using contemporary market economy language. That argument aside, I hope readers show me a little grace and mercy and focus on the points I am trying to make, as opposed to getting sidetracked by the market metaphor.
2. Bibby, 1999.
3. Bibby, 1994.
4. Posterski, Grainger, and Stiller, 2002:3.
5. Cited in *Flash Stories of Impact*. The Leadership Centre Willow Creek Canada, May 2003:1.

References

Ambrose, John E. (ed.).
    1997   *Seed that Dies to Rise: Lenten Reflections on Voices United.* Toronto: United Church Publishing House.

Anglican Church of Canada
    2004   *Serving God's World, Strengthening the Church, A Framework for a Common Journey in Christ, 2005-2010.* Toronto: General Synod of the Anglican Church of Canada, March.

Anthony, Lorrayne
    2003a   "The Force apparently with many Canadians." Ottawa: CP story in the *Toronto Star*, May 13.
    2003b   "Atheism growing across Canada, StatsCan shows." Ottawa CP story in the *Toronto Star*, May 13.

Baum, Gregory
    2002   "New Understanding of Mission." *Catholic New Times*, May 5.

Bellah, Robert, Richard Madsen, William Sullivan, Ann Swidler, and Steven Tipton
    1985   *Habits of the Heart.* New York: Harper and Row.

Berger, Peter L.
    1961   *The Noise of Solemn Assemblies.* Garden City, NY: Doubleday.

Berry, Carmen Renee
    2003   *The Unauthorized Guide to Choosing a Church.* Wheaton, IL: Brazos Press.

Berton, Pierre
    1982   *Why We Act Like Canadians.* Toronto: McClelland and Stewart.

Bibby, Reginald
    1986   *Anglitrends.* Toronto: Anglican Diocese of Toronto.
    1987   *Fragmented Gods: The Poverty and Potential of Religion in Canada.* Toronto: Irwin.
    1993   *Unknown Gods: The Ongoing Story of Religion in Canada.* Toronto: Stoddart.
    1994   *Unitrends.* Toronto: United Church of Canada.
    1995a   *There's God to be More! Connecting Churches and Canadians.* Winfield, BC: Wood Lake Books.
    1995b   *EvangelTrends.* Toronto: Evangelical Fellowship of Canada.
    1998   The PCPA Congregational Resource Study: Summary Report. St. Louis: Protestant Church-Owned Publishers Association.

1999   *The AllianceFuture Survey Summary Report.* Toronto: Christian and Missionary Alliance.

2001   *Canada's Teens: Today, Yesterday, and Tomorrow.* Toronto: Stoddart.

2002   *Restless Gods: The Renaissance of Religion in Canada.* Toronto: Stoddart/Novalis.

2004   *The Future Families Project: A Preliminary Analysis.* Ottawa: Vanier Institute of the Family.

Bird, John

2003   "Anglicans on the Edge." *The United Church Observer,* December.

Bott, Richard

2003   "A Ministry of Connection." *Exchange,* United Church of Canada, Fall.

Bradley, Ian

2000   *Celtic Christian Communities: Live the Tradition.* Kelowna: Northstone.

Brouillette, Marg

2002   "Montreal Mega-Church Multiplies Ministries." *Christian Week,* March.

Buchanan, Marg

2003   "Is Quebec Still a Mission Field?" *Christian Week,* May 13.

Burton, Anthony

1995   "Worship in Spirit and Truth: Designing Worship for Today's Church." In George Egerton (ed.). *Anglican Essentials: Reclaiming Faith Within the Anglican Church of Canada.* Toronto: Anglican Book Centre.

Byars, Ronald P.

2002   *The Future of Protestant Worship: Beyond the Worship Wars.* Philadelphia: Westminster John Knox Press.

Callaway, Tim

2002   "Congregation Donates $100,000 to Cross-City Mega-Church." *Christian Week,* March 5.

2003   "Break Forth Conference 'Life-Changing'." *Christian Week,* February 18.

Carroll, Colleen

2002   *The New Faithful: Why Young Adults Are Embracing Christian Orthodoxy.* Chicago: Loyola Press.

Catto, Susan

2003   "In Search of the Spiritual." *Time,* November 24:72-80.

Chattaway, Peter

2004   "Passion Piques Interest and Raises Eyebrows." *Christian Week,* February 17.

Cote, Richard

2003   *Lazarus! Come Out: Why Faith Needs Imagination.* Ottawa: Novalis.

Coupar, Regina

2002   *The Art of Soul: An Artist's Guide to Spirituality.* Ottawa: Novalis.

2004   *The Seeker's Heat: Meditations Inspired by the Book of Psalms.* Lethbridge: Blue Gamma Publications Corp.

Couto, Joe

2000   "Ethnic Korean Churches Thrive in Canada." *Faith Today,* May/June: 18-20.

Cox, Harvey
    1995   *Fire from Heaven: The Rise of Pentecostal Spirituality and the Reshaping of Religion in the Twenty-First Century.* Reading, MA: Perseus Books.

Czegledi, Jim
    2002   "The Unchurched – Where Are the People Going?" *Equip*, Presbyterian Church in Canada, August:5.

D'Antonio, William V., James D. Davidson, Dean R, Hoge, and Katherine Meyer
    2001   *American Catholics: Gender, Generation, and Commitment.* Walnut Creek, CA: Alta Mira Press.

Davidson, Jane
    2002a   "Carey, Ingham Quarrel Over Communion's Unity. *Anglican Journal*, November.
    2002b   "Youth Termed First Priority: Anglicans Polled on Their Church." *Anglican Journal*, December.
    2003a   "Ottawa Youth Group Just a Bunch of Holy Terrors." *Anglican Journal*, May.
    2003b   "Committee Examines Anglican Identity." *Anglican Journal*, May.

denBok, Connie
    2003a   "Where is Jesus Going? Something Has Shifted in the United Church of Canada." *Fellowship*, March:18-20.
    2003b   "What is Natural Church Development?" *Good Idea!* Wycliffe College Institute of Evangelism, Spring:1-2,6.

De Santis, Solange
    2003   "Whither the Downtown Montreal Churches?" *Anglican Journal*, May.
    2004   "Evangelism Not So Scary After All." *Anglican Journal*, January.

Dold, Patricia A.
    2000   "A Spiritual Journey Walking the Labyrinth." *Exchange*, Fall.

Doucette, Jeff
    2004   "Priestly Laryngitis: Moving Beyond Fear." *Catholic New Times*, March 21.

Duncan, Muriel
    2003   "Same Sex Marriage: 'The Table is Open for All'." *The United Church Observer*, October.

Emberley, Peter C.
    2002   *Divine Hunger: Canadians on Spiritual Walkabout.* Toronto: Harper Collins.

Galloway, Gloria
    2003   "Muslims outnumber Jews in Canada." *The Globe and Mail*, May 14.

Gatehouse, Jonathon
    2002   "A Church in Denial." *Maclean's*, July 22:22-26.

Gillis, Charlie
    2004   "Rude Awakening." *Maclean's*, April 5:28-32.

Glatz, Carol
    2004   "Love, Courage to Drive Evangelization." CNS story in the *Prairie Messenger*, March 17.

Glen, Bill
    2004   "Anglican-RC Relationships Rosy – Vatican Official." *Western Catholic Reporter*, February 16.

Gonzalez, Ramon
    2003   "Mannafest Rocks Teens' World." *Western Catholic Reporter*, September 22.
    2004   "Catholic Youth Suit Up for God." *Western Catholic Reporter*, February 9.

Grant, George Webster
    1988   *The Church in the Canadian Era.* Expanded edition. Burlington: Welch Publishing Company.

Greeley, Andrew
    1972   *The Denominational Society.* Glenview, IL: Scott Foresman.
    2004   "Theological Worlds Divide Younger and Older Clergy." *Prairie Messenger*, February 4.

Grossman, Cathy Lynn
    2002   "Charting the Unchurched in America." *USA Today*, March 7.

Gruending, Dennis
    1996   *Revival: Canada's Christian Churches.* Video. Ottawa: Carleton University.

Hadaway, C. Kirk and Penny Long Marler
    1993   "All in the Family: Religious Mobility in America." *Review of Religious Research* 35:97-116.

Hall, Douglas John
    1989   *The Future of the Church.* Toronto: United Church Publishing House.
    2000   "The United Church of Canada: A Religious Drama in Three Acts." *Theological Digest and Outlook* 15:42-44.

Harpur, Tom
    2004   *The Pagan Christ: Recovering the Lost Light.* Toronto: Thomas Allen.

Harvey, Bob
    2000   *The Future of Religion: Interviews With Christians on the Brink.* Ottawa: Novalis.

Helmers, Randy
    2002   From Lamentation to Celebration. *Exchange*, Spring:28-33.

Henry, Fred
    2001   "Spirituality Shallow Without Religion." *Western Catholic Reporter*, July 2.

Higgins, Michael W. and Douglas R. Letson
    2002   *Power and Peril: The Catholic Church at the Crossroads.* Toronto: Harper Collins.

Hill, John B.
    2003   "Rethinking the Church's Involvement in Weddings." *Liturgy Canada*, 9:1,3-5.

Hybels, Bill and Mark Mittelberg
    1995   *Becoming a Contagious Christian.* Grand Rapids: Zondervan.
    2002   *Courageous Leadership.* Grand Rapids: Zondervan.

Irvine, Andrew
    2001   "Small Churches – Being True to Who We Are." *Envision*, Fall:2-5.

Jantz, Harold
  1999a   "Keeping Company With One Another." *Faith Today,* May/June:20-31.
  1999b   "Catholics and Pentecostals in Lively Debate." *Faith Today,* May/June:23.

Johnstone, Meg
  2002   "Chinese Churches Thrive." *BC Christian News,* April:4-5.

Kelley, Dean
  1972   *Why Conservative Churches Are Growing.* New York: Harper and Row.

Knechtel, Ardith
  2001   "A 'W[a]rm' Experience!" *Fellowship,* June:4-7.

Larmondin, Leanne
  2002a   "New West Approves Same-Sex Blessings." *Anglican Journal,* September.

Larmondin, Leanne
  2002b   "Communion Reacts to Controversial Decision." *Anglican Journal,* September.

Larmondin, Leanne and Solange De Santis
  2002   "Same-sex Decision Proves Costly." *Anglican Journal,* September.

Liesch, Barry
  2001   *The New Worship: Straight Talk on Music and the Church.* Grand Rapids, MI: Baker Book House.

Lowes, Carol
  2000   "Churches Launch Joint Ad Campaign." *Faith Today,* May/June:15-16.
  2003   "Toronto Pub Puts Alpha Course on Tap." *Christian Week,* April 15:1,6.

McKim, Mark
  1998   "Evangelical Worship Fosters Secularism." *Faith Today,* January/February:45.

Meed Ward, Marianne
  1999   "Tears That Confront Us: Canada's Residential Schools Legacy and the Dream of Reconciliation." *Envision,* Summer 2000:1-6.

Milne, Mike
  2002a   "Letting Go of the Real Estate." *The United Church Observer,* April.
  2002b   "An Oasis in the Inner-City." *The United Church Observer,* May.
  2003a   "For Fun and Fund-Raising, the Play's the Thing." *The United Church Observer,* May.
  2003b   "A Developing Controversy: To Build or Not to Build?" *The United Church Observer,* July-August.
  2003c   "Local Churches and Same-Sex Marriage: Debate or Wait?" *The United Church Observer,* November.
  2004   "Do-It-Yourself-Renewal." *The United Church Observer,* March.

Nol, Mark A.
  1992   *A History of Christianity in the United States and Canada.* Grand Rapids, MI: Eerdmans.

Oden, Thomas C.

2002 *The Rebirth of Orthodoxy: Signs of New Life in Christianity.* San Francisco: Harpers.

Orr, Edwin J.

1936 *Times of Refreshing: 10,000 Miles of Miracle Through Canada.* Toronto: Evangelical Publishers.

Overholt, L. David and James Penner

2004 *Soul Searching the Millennial Generation: Strategies for Youth Workers.* 2nd edition. Ottawa: Novalis.

Paddey, Patricia L.

2003 "Christian Leaders Connect." *Christian Week,* February 18.

2004 "Passion Spurs Community Outreach." *Christian Week,* March 16.

Perras, Michael

2003 "Youth Ministry Seminar Draws from Across Canada." *Western Catholic Reporter,* September 22.

Plug, Rudy

2001 "Why Stay?" *Fellowship,* June:24.

Posterski, Donald C. and Irwin Barker

1993 *Where's a Good Church?* Winfield, BC: Wood Lake Books.

Posterski, Don

1999 "A Conversation with Vern Heidebrecht and Bill Hybels." *Envision,* Fall:8-10.

Posterski, Don

2000 "A Conversation With Elijah Harper." *Envision,* Spring:10-11.

Posterski, Don with Brett Grainger and Karen Stiller

2002 "Spiritual Styles = Leadership Challenges." *Envision,* Autumn:1-9.

Posterski, Don and Andrew Grenville

2004a "Like Thy Neighbour? The Religious Differences Between Canada and the U.S." *Envision,* Spring:8-9.

2004b "The Complicated and Irrepressible Canadian Church." *Envision,* Spring:2-6.

Preiner, Sally Edmonds

2001 *Stained Glass, Sweet Grass, Hosannas, & Songs: A Snapshot of Anglican Issues and Visions in Canada.* Toronto: Anglican Book Centre.

Pyles, Franklin

2003 "Cathedrals of the New Century." *Christian Week,* Spring:1-2.

Reardon, J. Ashe

2002 "The Cardinal and the *Globe.*" *Religion in the News,* Spring:5,28.

Redman, Robb

2002 *The Great Worship Awakening: Singing a New Song in the Postmodern Church.* San Francisco: Jossey-Bass.

Roof, Wade Clark

1999 *Spiritual Marketplace: Baby Boomers and the Remaking of American Religion.*

Princeton, NJ: Princeton University Press.

Salutin, Rick
    2002   "Hopalong Cassidy and John Paul." *Globe and Mail,* July 26.

Sartison, Telmor
    1998   *The Voice of One: A Continuing Journey in Faith.* Winnipeg: Evangelical Lutheran Church in Canada.

Schaller, Lyle E.
    1995   *The New Reformation.* Nashville: Abingdon.

Schultz, Raymond L.
    2004   "Epiphany: The Day the Lights Went On." Sermon delivered February 1. *From the Bishop's Desk.* Winnipeg: Evangelical Lutheran Church in Canada website: www.elcic.ca.

Schultze, Quentin
    2004   *High-Tech Worship?: Using Presentational Techniques Wisely.* Grand Rapids, MI: Baker.

Schwarz, Christian A.
    1996   *Natural Church Development: A Guide to Eight Essential Qualities of Healthy Churches.* Saint Charles, IL: ChurchSmart Resources.

Silk, Mark
    2002   "The Media vs. the Church." *Religion in the News,* Spring:1-2

Sinclair, Donna
    2002   "Brave New Worship." *The United Church Observer,* September.
    2003a   "Talking Our Way Toward God." *The United Church Observer,* July-August.
    2003b   "Listening to Jesus in the 21st Century." *The United Church Observer,* September.

Sinclair, Donna and Christopher White
    2003   *Emmaus Road: Churches Making Their Way Forward.* Kelowna: Wood Lake Books.

Sison, Marites N.
    2005   "Task Force Queries All Sides in Troubled Diocese." *Anglican Journal,* February.

Snopek, Roxanne
    2003   "Pastor Witnesses in Non-Church Weddings." *BC Christian News,* February:11.

Stackhouse, John G. Jr.
    2003   *Evangelical Landscapes: Facing Critical Issues of the Day.* Grand Rapids, MI: Baker Academic.

Stark, Rodney and Roger Finke
    2000   *Acts of Faith: Explaining the Human Side of Religion.* University of California Press.

Stirk, Frank
    2003   "Get Back to the Basics, National Church Planters Told." *Christian Week,* December 16.
    2004   "Good Church Health Equals Growth – Survey." *Christian Week,* February 27.

Struch, Joanne
    2004   "Canadian Catholicism Marked by Multiculturalism." CCN story in the *Prairie Messenger*, March 17.

Todd, Douglas
    1996   *Brave Souls: Writers and Artists Wrestles with God, Love, Death, and the Things That Matter.* Toronto: Stoddart.

Valpy, Michael
    2002   "Same-Sex Dispute Saddens Archbishop." *Globe and Mail*, June 19:A3.

Walker, Melissa
    2003   "Young, Searching and New to the Pews." *The United Church Observer*, September.

Walsh, Andrew
    2002   "The Scandal of Secrecy." *Religion in the News*, Spring:3-4, 5-9, 30-31.
    2003   "A World of Hurt." *Religion in the News*, Spring:11-12,24.

Ward, Michael
    2003   "Empowering Leadership." *Fellowship Magazine*, September:4-7.

Warren, Rick
    1995   *The Purpose Driven Church: Growth Without Compromising Your Message & Mission.* Grand Rapids, MI: Zondervan.
    2002   *The Purpose Driven Life.* Grand Rapids, MI: Zondervan.

Weatherbe, Steve
    2003   "Let's Work Together, Says Mainse." *Western Catholic Reporter*, July 21.

Wente, Margaret
    2004   "Passion Bashin' is in Fashion." *Globe and Mail*, March 20.

Wilson, David
    2003   "A Sanctuary from the Streets." *The United Church Observer*, May.

Winseman, Albert L.
    2003   "Baby Steps Toward Healing the Catholic Church." *The Gallup Brain*, June 24.

Woods, C. Jeff
    1996   *Congregational Megatrends.* Washington: The Alban Institute.

Woolever, Cynthia and Deborah Bruce
    2002   *A Field Guide to U.S. Congregations: Who's Going Where and Why.* Louisville: John Knox Press.

Yaworski, Kiply Lukan
    2004   "Christian Community Vision Shared." CCN story in the *Prairie Messenger*, March 17.

Index

Note: Page numbers followed by "n" refer to endnotes.